Mass Fatality
and Casualty
Incidents
A Field Guide

Mass Fatality
and Casualty
Incidents
A Field Guide

by
Robert A. Jensen

CRC Press
Taylor & Francis Group
Boca Raton   London   New York

CRC Press is an imprint of the
Taylor & Francis Group, an **informa** business

Library of Congress Cataloging-in-Publication Data

Jensen, Robert A. (Robert Andrew)
  Mass fatality and casualty incidents : a field guide / Robert A.
Jensen.
      p. cm.
  Includes bibliographical references and index.
  ISBN 0-8493-1295-7
  1. Forensic sciences Handbooks, manuals, etc. 2. Emergency
management Handbooks, manuals, etc. I. Title.
HV8073. J46 1999
363.34'81—dc21   97-38461
                                                                           CIP

This book contains information obtained from authentic and highly regarded sources. Reprinted material is quoted with permission, and sources are indicated. A wide variety of references are listed. Reasonable efforts have been made to publish reliable data and information, but the author and the publisher cannot assume responsibility for the validity of all materials or for the consequences of their use.

Visit the CRC Press Web site at www.crcpress.com

© 2000 by CRC Press

No claim to original U.S. Government works
International Standard Book Number 0-8493-1295-7
Library of Congress Card Number   97-38461
Printed in the United States of America   9 0
Printed on acid-free paper

Preface

Preserve the dignity of the deceased, while meeting the rights and needs of the living, and the requirements of governmental investigations.

Simply put, that is the successful resolution to a mass fatality incident. It is not one person's job, but rather the combined results of a team of people representing several disciplines and agencies, both public and private, who have—or should have—the same goal. The problems begin when one or more members of the team, by lack of understanding, either place their agencies' need at a higher priority or fail to accept that all requirements are valid.

What often causes this "lack of understanding" is a combination of many system failures. The first is often the most obvious, and that is the lack of a workable and realistic response plan. The second failure is a lack of training, from the individual responder to the incident managers. The third is the dearth of experienced subject-matter experts to help develop response plans and training. The fourth failure is jurisdictional parochialism, with some agencies or individuals simply not wanting to work toward a successful solution.

This guide was developed to answer that lack of understanding.

It is organized and presented to provide both a step-by-step understanding and to serve as a tabbed ready reference should the need arise. It is based on the actual response and study of several mass fatality incidents.

A key point to remember is that this is only a guide; unfortunately, I do not have a magic pill that will solve all incident problems. You are dealing with sudden and unexpected death, an emotional issue. No matter what action you take, some family members and others will not be satisfied and nothing you can do will make them satisfied—after all, they have lost their loved ones.

Your peace and satisfaction come when you can say, without hesitation, that you have done everything in your power to ensure that you and your agency's actions worked to preserve the dignity of the deceased, meet the rights and needs of the living, and the requirements of governmental investigations.

Robert Andrew Jensen

Introduction

This guide has been organized to provide you, the responder, with several tools to help you before, during, and after a mass fatality incident.

To begin with, I recommend reading through the entire guide. As you read, ask yourself how you or your agency would fit into the response. Make notes on questions to ask your counterparts in other agencies, and look critically at all areas.

The guide is organized as follows:

Within this section, I have included some very common, but very avoidable, misconceptions about a response operation that could become pitfalls. I have also included a section establishing common terminology and the importance of ensuring that all responders have the same understanding of certain key terms.

Chapter 1 provides some suggested strategies for senior leaders in overall incident management. Different management systems are detailed as well as the various roles of response agencies.

Chapter 2 provides a quick walk through the key points of establishing a mass fatality incident response. It also provides a quick look at the flow of decedent operations.

Chapter 3 provides details on how to manage and cope with the realities of your, your responders', and the community's response to mass death, and Chapter 4 takes a very detailed look at ways to meet various mandated laws and regulations with regard to exposure of bloodborne pathogens and hazardous materials.

Chapters 5 to 10 cover in detail the specific response actions in search and recovery of fatalities, the establishment and running of the morgue, recovery and handling of personal effects, family assistance, dealing with the media, and logistical support operations.

Chapter 11 provides an overview of the Federal Response Plan, various federal laws governing mass fatality incident response and how operations should proceed during a joint response.

Appendix A provides detailed forms that list equipment organized by response action, i.e., search and recovery equipment, morgue equipment, personal effects equipment and standard office equipment. Clearly, many agencies cannot and do not need to stockpile mass fatality incident response equipment, however, they should have a list of what's needed and where it can be acquired on short notice.

Appendix B provides a place to note local and national points of contacts, and a listing of reference books and specialized response organizations.

Some Common Misperceptions

As long as everyone knows his or her job we don't need to practice or meet before an incident.

As a responder or manager there is no greater concern than arriving at an incident and hearing the words, "Pleased to meet you." Although you may be familiar with the reputations of the others, you will not truly know their capabilities, have a feel for the way they will react to the incident, or their goals and motives in resolving the incident. In other words, you will probably have no comfort zone. Think of the opposite—arriving at an incident scene hearing the words, "Good to see you again." Seeing other responders and managers with whom you have attended training, and knowing that there is a common understanding of terminology and familiarity with work practices will go a long way in establishing a productive team spirit and setting a positive tone.

During a mass fatality incident people will be able to respond and perform in a way that is totally different from routine day-to-day functioning.

In a highly charged and emotional event such as a mass fatality incident, responders and managers will default to completing tasks in the manner to which they are most accustomed. For example, your office may have a routine day-to-day operational morgue protocol that specifies that certain actions happen in a specific order. However, if during a mass fatality incident you completely change that protocol, not only have you have inserted an additional stress factor, but you have greatly increased the chance for an error. It is best to train the way you operate and operate the way you train.

Tough realistic mass fatality incident training isn't needed; we do our job every day, so a mass fatality incident isn't that hard.

While it may be true for senior managers, leading a mass fatality incident response is not that difficult. But is a senior manager going to manage the incident and also do the response work? Probably not; the majority of tasks will most likely be done by less-experienced personnel. An obvious advantage of experience is that one has successfully completed the action previously or, if not completely successful, hopefully learned some key lessons from participating in the incident response. However, because repetitive mass fatality incidents in the same geographical area are fortunately rare, many people don't get actual experience. Therefore, when individuals participate in tough, realistic training, it provides them with a basis for establishing an understanding of what occurs at an incident and what their individual role in that incident is.

Author's note: During a response to a particularly devastating air crash, I had, as a matter of routine, set aside time every evening for one-on-one conversations (see Chapter 3) with subordinate managers and responders. I did this for several reasons, one of which was to ensure that people were doing okay and to find out what was going on from different levels. During one of these conversations, I spoke with one subordinate manager who confided that when he was first notified of the incident he was a little worried that he would not do well because he had never responded to a large plane crash before. However, he had also been through a complete, full-scale, three-day mass fatality incident exercise three months prior to this incident, and when he saw that the actual response to the incident was very similar to the training, he said he knew he could do it. He knew that because he knew what his role was and what to expect. He said nothing could be worse than the training exercise and he and everyone else had survived that.

During a mass fatality incident, rules go out the window.

Frankly, not only is the opposite true, but you will probably be surprised at the swift arrival and number of compliance inspectors who seem to arrive at about the same time you do. Although cumbersome and sometimes hard for us to accept, many Occupational Standards and Health Administration (OSHA) rules, whether enforced at the local, state, or national levels, serve to ensure that we as responders and managers are protected from unnecessary risks, even in unusual and catastrophic events. Indeed, while you may not agree with the standards, you have little choice but to follow them.

Adhering to the OSHA mandates actually becomes more important during a mass fatality incident response because there will be many people involved with incident response. Some will have no familiarity with standard preventive measures for exposure to bloodborne pathogens and hazardous materials. Knowing up front and accepting that the rules will be enforced and that everyone must follow them is just one more reason to develop and have a plan in place for response to a mass fatality incident.

During a mass fatality incident, I am able to buy whatever I need and worry about paying for it later.

Response to a mass fatality incident is not inexpensive. Smaller jurisdictions can see their entire annual budget wiped out in a mass fatality incident that lasts only three weeks. Presently, the federal government and at times, private industry involved in the incident, may provide reimbursement for some costs associated with the response. However, that is not always the case. Difficulties occur when an agency cannot account for the amounts spent. Careful accounting and controlled acquisition by a specified person are simple ways of ensuring that your agency can account for and document costs when applying for reimbursement.

No plan survives a mass fatality incident.

As you may have heard, "Failing to plan is planning to fail." When you plan ahead, you have the advantage of being able to think through actions and consider their consequences. You can review legal requirements and compare how your plan interfaces with other agencies to ensure your expectations are the same as theirs. Others will then have a reference to know what to expect from you. During the incident response, you will not have time to do those things, and, more important, everyone else will know what you are doing.

At a mass fatality incident mistakes happen, and that's okay.

Although few people believe that zero-defect environments exist, the reality is that response to a mass fatality incident must be a zero-defects environment. Errors, intentional or accidental, minor or not so minor, can cause additional distress to families, provide a foundation for questions of professional competence, and possibly lead to challenges during criminal proceedings or civil litigation. Almost all mass fatality incidents result in criminal prosecution and or civil litigation for the loss of family members.

Author's note: In a past incident, a fragment of a body was mistakenly included in a casket with a whole body. The mistake went unnoticed and could only be corrected by going to a family and asking for permission to exhume their relative and recover the fragment. Ramifications of this included additional distress to the surviving family members, questions in court about the true number of fatalities, and accusations of incompetence.

Mass fatality incidents are not political.

While that is true for most mass fatality incidents that result from a natural disaster, it is most certainly not true when dealing with deliberate incidents or major transportation accidents. The result of political involvement ranges from mere annoyance during the incident to far-reaching and impacting legislation.

During response to mass fatality incidents that occur as part of a larger natural disaster, the focus and attention will most likely be on the overall recovery effort and the actions being taken to help the living. However, when an incident is strictly a mass fatality incident, most of the attention will be on the incident response.

Everything is as it seems.
The same problems that plague us in day-to-day life also impact mass fatality incident response. Nothing in an incident should be taken for granted. No manifest is ever 100% accurate 100% of the time. Common problems are people using aliases (especially when traveling) and people claiming to be family when they are not. Rare, although not unheard of, in some cases enterprising criminals will use a mass fatality incident site as an area to get rid of a homicide victim.

During the response to a mass fatality incident you should question those things that you would normally question.

Terms and Definitions

To ensure a common base for understanding I have defined specific terms as they are used in this book.

Many problems and disagreements needlessly occur in the course of incident response when different responders disagree over a certain action based on the words used to describe that action, when in fact, they may both be talking about the same thing. This is just another reason that managers should plan and train together.

Mass Fatality Incident

What is a mass fatality incident? Is it a building bombed, with 169 killed; a commuter plane crash, with 49 killed; or a school bus hit by a train, with 10 killed?

The bombing certainly would be a mass fatality incident in any jurisdiction. However, the plane crash and bus accident may not be. A mass fatality incident is generally described as any event that produces more fatalities than can be handled using local resources. Additionally, the total number of deceased may not create a mass fatality incident. The manner in which death occurred and the resulting condition of the deceased are more important. One must also look at who the victims are. A school bus accident resulting in 10 students' being killed will certainly have a greater impact on the responders. It will also most likely have a longer lasting impact on the community, thereby falling under the heading of a mass fatality incident.

What actions are part of a mass fatality incident response? For the purposes of this manual they are the actions that begin once life and property preservation ceases and continue through to the release of the deceased and their accompanying personal effects to those individuals eligible to direct disposition and receive effects. Primary focus is on the following steps: search, recovery, medicolegal investigation, personal effects operations, family assistance operations, and media operations. Ancillary operations include logistics support, security, responder protection, and attitudes and coping with mass death.

The amount of time it takes to complete each action will again depend on the condition of the bodies and also on the level of action required for each operation. In other words, what is the goal relative to incident resolution? Is it complete identification of all fatalities and association of any human remains part recovered? Does it also include complete medicolegal autopsy, including determining manner, cause, and mechanism of death? What investigation reports will be required? These and others are all questions that will determine if an incident exceeds the capabilities of the local resources.

Medical Examiner

For sake of simplicity, I use the term Medical Examiner to represent the duly appointed or elected official of a county, state, territory, or federal department such as the Armed Forces Medical Examiner, who has the responsibility to investigate all unexpected deaths, homicides, and suicides. As most readers are no doubt aware, in the U.S. that could be a Coroner, Sheriff-Coroner, Coroner–Public Administrator, or Medical Examiner. Medical Examiners are, in most cases, medical doctors, and a good percentage are forensic pathologists.

In cases where the duly appointed authority is not a medical examiner, I strongly recommend that the appointed authority share the key decision making with a forensic pathologist, who is most likely already on staff, or who serves as a contractor who routinely performs autopsies for the jurisdiction.

Medicolegal Death Investigation

This is a rather new term, but it will—and should be—established as the standard for death investigation. As noted by Dr. Joseph H. Davis, in *Medicolegal Death Investigation – Treatises In The Forensic Sciences,* (Yale H. Caplan, Ph.D., Ed., page 79, The Forensic Sciences Foundation Press, 1997) a medicolegal death investigation will: "Provide answers to questions of what factors served to cause the fatal incident or interfered with survival.

Final conclusions of cause, manner and circumstances of death must rest upon a firm correlative bank of pertinent data, both autopsy and circumstantial derived."

The key point here is that medical examiners, working in a vacuum by confining their work to an autopsy suite, may render a report that is not accurate. Experience has proven that medical examiners who actively participate and begin their involvement early in the response can and do render accurate, complete, and defendable reports.

Morgue

A location or locations for the establishment of positive identification of the deceased, performance of autopsies if required, completion of individual case file documentation, and completion of detailed death incident reports, and if so organized, aftercare tasks such as embalming and casketing for return to persons authorized to direct disposition.

Identification

In a mass fatality incident the identification of the deceased will most likely prove to be the most problematic issue for the medical examiner. Even if autopsies are not conducted, all attempts at establishing a positive identification must be made. The number of resources required for identification is based solely on the incident dynamics.

A key point to remember is that many in the public are not aware of the physical trauma caused by a sudden catastrophic event such as a transportation accident or building collapse. Many people still believe that one must just pick up a wallet or purse and match whatever photo identification is present to the nearest remains and instantly you have positive ID. This misconception is not limited to the victims' family members, but may apply even to those who may be in charge or able to influence event response.

Author's note: Within hours of a plane crash in which a very senior government official and several others were killed, a question repeatedly asked by top level government personnel was had the official been recovered and identified. This crash had occurred on the border of two formally warring countries and the crash had barely been located when the question was first asked. Even after the decision had been made to effect the recovery and conduct identification work back in the U.S., the question was still being asked. Obviously, the people asking the question did not understand the process of identification. What makes this interesting is that some of them were senior planners, who had never needed or bothered to understand the response system.

You as the responder can ignore these questions, as well as the decisions and criticism these people will make. However, a better solution is to include in your prewritten mass fatality incident press releases a short statement explaining the identification process.

Types of identification often fall into one of the following categories:

Positive or Confirmatory Identification. Occurs when antemortem (existing before death) and postmortem (created as part of the medicolegal autopsy or medicolegal investigation) records are compared and enough specific unique data markers match to conclude that the records were created from the same individual. Furthermore, no irreconcilable differences are established. Unique data markers include fingerprints, footprints, DNA, MtDNA, dentition, and previously diagnosed medical conditions.

Possible, Presumptive, or Believed-To-Be (BTB) Identification. Occurs when several individual factors are considered and, although no single factor alone justifies the establishment of identification, taken together the factors are sufficient for a possible or presumptive identification. Factors include identifiable personal effects, visual recognition, racial characteristics, age, sex, stature, anomalies, or individualizing skeletal traits (handedness, parity body build) and photo superimposition.

Exclusion. Occurs when all deceased in a definable category, such as male or female, have been identified, all surviving victims accounted for, the BTB identification has been verified as a person who was known to be involved with the death incident, and the only remaining deceased could not be anyone else. For example, an adult male who had a confirmed flight reservation for the aircraft that crashed and has not been seen since the accident may be identified and matched to the accounted name when only one adult male body has not been identified through any other means and all other adult males are accounted for.

Personal Effects (see Chapter 7)

Personal effects are those items that we carry in our pockets, purses, briefcases, backpacks, and similar devices, and that we travel with and carry as "luggage." The value of personal effects in the identification process is listed above. However, far greater than their intrinsic value is the return of personal effects to those persons eligible to receive them, such as family members. The sentimental value of these items, no matter how small or trivial to a responder, should not be underestimated.

Unfortunately, in a mass fatality incident, death is not neat; most remains are not viewable and since the death was unexpected and occurred way from family members, there was no chance to say good-bye. Personal effects give the families a tangible reminder of their loved ones, in that this was the last item to be with their relatives when they died.

Because of this importance, I strongly recommend that the responsibility to effect disposition of personal effects be turned over to an experienced private contractor. Thus, personal effects operations include the search, recovery (which can also be done by a private party), processing, and turnover to a third party.

Remains or Fragments

For years, mass fatality incident responders have been confronted with the problem of defining what remains are. Intact or largely intact bodies are certainly properly classified as remains, but what about a part of human body? Should that single portion be called remains?

The challenge is that when you are conducting a search and recovery operation or doing preliminary mass fatality incident morgue work you will not know if that part you are working with is all that is left of a body or if it is one of several portions that will be recovered.

To keep it simple, I use the term remains to describe any part of a human body recovered.

Viewable or Non-Viewable

Remains or fragments are considered viewable when there is a good chance that after care may allow viewing of them. They are considered non-viewable when there is little chance that after-care services will allow viewing.

Decedent Operations

This term is used to describe any activities involving the search, recovery, medicolegal investigation, after care, and disposition of any deceased person.

Aftercare

A term used to describe any of the following activities, which usually occur after the completion of any medicolegal investigation of the remains: embalming, postmortem reconstructive surgery, casketing, cremation, and interment.

The Author

Robert A. Jensen, BS, has extensive "hands-on" military and civilian experience in his dealings with mass fatality incidents. He provided leadership and management during such high-profile situations as the Oklahoma City bombing and Secretary of Commerce Ron Brown's plane crash in Croatia, following which he led and directed the on-ground search, recovery, and evacuation of all victims.

Jensen has also:

- Successfully led a 175-person U.S. Army company, directing multiple real-world troop deployments supporting the search, recovery, and repatriation of deceased military and civilian personnel.
- Planned and executed the fatality support plans for the U.S. mission to Bosnia–Herzegovina, serving as the U.S. representative to NATO joint boards, and developing fatality support plans for all nations involved.
- Developed, planned, and executed the mass fatality portion of a major exercise involving the recovery of nuclear-contaminated remains, successfully culminating in a multi-million dollar two-week disaster drill involving more than 2000 people from 27 federal, state, and local agencies.
- Served as the lead project officer in developing the U.S. military's first and only Joint Manual for mortuary affairs support.
- Provided technical assistance to various states on responding to air crashes, natural disasters, and hazardous-material accident-preparedness response.
- Developed and conducted law enforcement and medical examiner training on the recovery and processing of multiple-death crime scenes or unusual-death investigations and mass-fatality-incident response.
- Been called upon to provide detailed technical presentations to members of Congress and staff members of the Joint Chiefs of Staff, to Governors, Secretaries, U.S. military general and flag officers, foreign military general officers, U.S. State Department counselors, medical examiners, and emergency-response planners.

Jensen is a member of the American Academy of Forensic Sciences, the National Emergency Managers Association, the International Association of Emergency Managers, and the National Foundation for Mortuary Care. He is also the director of planning and training for Kenyon International Emergency Services, Inc., a worldwide leader in mass fatality incident response.

Robert Jensen has written several papers, lectured, and served as a consultant on the subject of mass fatality incidents.

Acknowledgments

Clearly, such an undertaking as completing this guide is not the work of just one person. I have been fortunate throughout my life to have worked with some of the best people in the world. In many cases, these people have served as my mentors, and have provided me with knowledge, the ability to learn from my mistakes and to know right from wrong, and, most importantly, with the determination to keep going no matter what the odds.

I cannot possibly list every person who has been of assistance in the completion of this guide; however, I would be remiss if I did not attempt to mention at least a few of them. I must express my thanks to my beloved grandfather John Armstrong; James Bouley; Dr. Faruk Presswalla; Dr. Marcella Fierro; and the entire staff of the office of the Chief Medical Examiner, the Commonwealth of Virginia; the past, present, and future soldiers of the U.S. Army's 54th Quartermaster Company (Mortuary Affairs) and all mortuary affairs soldiers; LTC Terry Clemons; LTC (ret)Ted Leemann; and LTC Marilyn Brooks.

I must also mention Kenyon International Emergency Services, Inc., the world's premier mass fatality incident response company for the use of several photographs in this guide. Furthermore, Kenyon's entire staff has been more than generous in its comments. In particular, I thank Mike Spinello, John Warren, Nealan Kerwin, Tina Allen, Donna Armstrong, Peter Gregory, Chris Statham, Jan Gordon, and Ken Tipton.

I must thank, also, my ever-optimistic editor Becky A. McEldowney and the entire production department at CRC Press, who have more patience than anyone is entitled to. Simply put, this guide would not have been completed without their support.

And, last but by no means least, my long-suffering wife and daughter, who tolerate my far-too-frequent and unplanned absences only to be asked to put up with my late nights and weekends locked away typing when I am home.

Dedication

This guide is dedicated to the victims—those we represent because they can no longer represent themselves—to the living: the families, survivors, and communities whose lives will never be the same—and to the responders: those who unselfishly place their own lives and emotions on hold to help others.

Table of Contents

7 Personal Effects Operations

8 Family Assistance

9 Media Operations

Incident Management 1

Who's in Charge?—Managing the Unmanageable

One of the most commonly asked questions at a mass fatality incident site is who's in charge? The answer will depend on when and whom you ask. To make matters worse, more than one person might claim to be in charge at the same time. In reality, during a mass fatality incident no one person is truly in charge of the entire response or operation. Each responding agency should have a leader, and all agency leaders should work together to ensure that the common goals are achieved without undue expense to any one area.

What are the common goals? Simply put, there are three goals in responding to a mass fatality incident.

1. Preserve the dignity of the deceased. As a mass fatality incident responder, you are responsible for ensuring that the rights of the deceased are protected; you're their advocate. They can no longer speak for themselves in demanding justice and proper treatment; you must do it for them. The deceased should be treated with respect and afforded dignity at all times.

2. Meet the rights and needs of the living. As a mass fatality incident responder, you must complete your job so that the concerns, cares, and desires of the living are met.

Who is meant by the living? They are the families, and they often want very little. In fact, they often want only to have their loved one's remains returned as soon as possible; to have their bodies treated with respect; to be given the option of deciding about receiving their relatives' personal effects;

1

to participate in decisions about mass burials and memorials; and, when they are at the incident site, they want their physical needs, such as food and shelter, taken care of.

The living are also the communities; the high school that loses most of its French club or sports team; or the town that just happens to be where the incident occurred. Each "community" will want to play a role in the response and should be involved, even if it is only to be afforded the opportunity to grieve. They would like to be able to return to a routine as soon as possible.

The living are also the survivors, those lucky individuals who happen to be in the right seat at the right time and survived just because it wasn't their time. After medical care, they will also have needs; in some cases, they may have lost loved ones in the incident, and they will want their personal effects back. They will also likely want to participate in memorials and remembrances.

3. Follow the requirements of government investigations. In almost any incident that occurs today, either criminal or civil litigation will most likely be the end result. Because of that, complex and lengthy investigations by various agencies and forensic disciplines are often undertaken. Additionally, in some transportation accidents, detailed investigation will be undertaken to find the exact cause of the incident to ensure that lessons learned can be applied to future operations to avoid any recurrence.

Each responding agency will have as its primary mission one or more of those goals. The challenge is to ensure that the responding agency leaders do not take actions that hamper or impede the other agencies. In mass fatality incidents, every action impacts another action. Once actions are completed, it is almost impossible to go back and start over.

Therefore, successful incident management will depend on the coordination, cooperation, and teamwork of the responding agency leaders.

Incident Management Systems

For many years, the only standardized incident management system was the Incident Command System (ICS), which for the most part has worked well. However, in mass fatality incidents and other incidents in which many local, state, and federal government agencies, as well as private industry respond it has not been as successful. The scope of such incidents required a greater management system. In response to that requirement, the Standardized Emergency Management System (SEMS) was developed.

Currently, many agencies still prefer to use only ICS. Used alone and as currently organized, I do not personally think it is the best system. I recommend a combination of both ICS and SEMS. Therefore, I will discuss those areas of ICS that work well in mass fatality incident response.

Incident Command System (ICS)

The ICS was developed in the 1960s. It first came into use in California, and was later adopted for use by the U.S. National Fire Academy and the U.S. Emergency Management Institute, and has become a standard in the National Fire Protection Association. It was developed to eliminate the mass confusion in response to several large brush and woodland fires.

In the U.S., the ICS has become the most common method of incident management. For quite some time it was the only standardized method of incident management. Today, many regulations require that emergency response departments have written plans for ICS, train their members on ICS and when responding use ICS.

The ICS components that work well for a mass fatality incident are:

- Common terminology—Everyone must understand and use basic terms.
- Modular system—You implement only those functions that are needed at a particular incident.
- Integrated communications—Everyone must understand how to communicate and with whom they should communicate.
- Span of control—At any one time supervisors should only be responsible for up to seven people.
- Comprehensive resource management—Used to group common types of resources.

Those components, when followed, work very well and contribute to the overall success of mass fatality incident response.

In addition to the components of ICS, there are five major functional areas. They are:

1. Management
2. Operations
3. Planning
4. Logistics
5. Finance

As the standardized emergency management system also uses the functional areas, I will discuss them in the next section.

Standardized Emergency Management System (SEMS)

The SEMS was developed in the early 1990s. It, like the ICS, was developed and started in California. It was also following the confusion created during response to a very large, deadly, and destructive urban firestorm.

Currently, only the State of California mandates its use during disasters. However, like the ICS, its usefulness and success in incident management is causing other states and jurisdictions to look at adopting SEMS. I believe it is only a matter of time before it is the standard.

The goal of SEMS was to organize the response to any incident starting with the lowest level of resources and support required, escalating in a controlled manner to draw on the nearest available resources through a system of mutual aid and inter-agency cooperation.

The SEMS incorporates the following:

Incident Command System—For use within each responding agency and those components that are applicable to the overall management.

Multi- and Inter-Agency Coordination—Although many agencies with different missions will respond to an incident, and some will have multiple missions, all must be coordinated to focus on the overall mission.

Mutual Aid—Recognizing that neighboring jurisdictions have multiple agencies that provide the same type of service, such as various city fire departments in one county, those agencies should pool their resources to provide assistance to the affected region.

Operational Area Concept—SEMS has divided the response into key areas, beginning with:

1. Operational Areas

Operational areas are described in terms of the jurisdiction level of the primary responding agencies.

- **Field**—The actual incident location and response activities
- **Local**—The lowest level of response, usually a city or county (for medical examiner operations)
- **Operational Area**—Defined as a county, and encompasses the entire incident area.
- **Regional**—The State of California was divided into various regions. Within the regions, one county was appointed the regional coordinator, who is responsible for receiving all requests for support and either

providing support from within his region or asking the state for assistance. For example, when any county within a region has an incident that they cannot handle with local resources, they contact the regional coordinator. The regional coordinator then looks to the other counties within the region; if none can provide the additional support the request is forwarded to the state level.

- **State**—At the state level, the State Emergency Operations Center, or State Office of Emergency Services, receives requests from the regional coordinator and determines if other regions or any of the various state agencies can provide support. If so, they are asked to provide the support. If they cannot provide the support, the state will then ask the federal government.

2. Functional Areas

To better manage the incident, SEMS incorporated the ICS functional areas into the overall management of the incident.

- **Management**—Both ICS And SEMS use the word "command," but I believe the word "manage" better represents the actual function. The management function encompasses the overall coordination of the incident, to include the leadership of the various response areas.

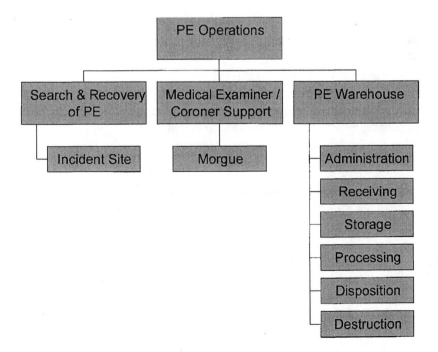

Figure 1.1 Organizational chart of overall management of mass fatality incident.

- **Operations** (see Figure 1.1)—The operations section should coordinate and provide direction and information to all the response areas. In a mass fatality incident those areas are:

  a. Overall incident management operations
  b. Law enforcement operations (which include security, incident investigations, and medical examiner support)
  c. Family assistance operations
  d. Decedent operations (which include search and recovery and mass fatality incident morgue)
  e. Media operations
  f. Personal effects (which include search and recovery, personal effects warehouse, and medical examiner support)

- Planning and intelligence

The planning and intelligence cell should be looking toward the next level of operations to anticipate what will be occurring next. They should work very closely with the operations section to ensure that future operations can go forward.

- Logistics

The logistics section focuses on coordinating support to response areas. In a mass fatality incident in which a complete logistical support operation has been established, this function should move to that location.

- Finance and Administration

The finance and administration section provides administrative support to the incident management operations center and also tracks the expenditure of funds for all response areas. Just as with logistics, in a mass fatality incident in which a complete logistical support operation has been established, this function should move to that location.

3. **Management Systems Applied to Mass Fatality Incidents**

Your response to a mass fatality incident should be to use a functional approach and develop those response areas that you will need. The response areas are those that provide actual resources to the response:

a. Incident management operations
b. Law enforcement operations (which include security and incident investigations)
c. Family assistance operations

    d. Decedent operations (which includes search and recovery and mass fatality incident morgue)
    e. Media operations
    f. Personal effects (which includes search and recovery and personal effects warehouse)
    g. Logistics operations

Each response area should be headed by a primary or lead agency, which should be selected based on its resources and capabilities in the particular response area or by legal mandate. Other agencies should be designated as support agencies for one or more of the response areas based on their resources and capabilities to support the response area.

Each response area should then be divided into separate areas with primary agencies or personnel appointed to head that area. Again supporting agencies should also be designated.

4. Response Areas

The following response areas apply only to those activities that occur once lifesaving and property preservation are complete. You may not need every area for each incident.

Some basic thoughts:

- You should establish only those areas that are required.
- Limit the number of support personnel to those who are truly needed.
- If you are able to rotate personnel without degrading your operation, do it. Not only does it help with reducing responder stress, it also provides a way for you to train and gain experienced personnel.

Incident Management Operation Centers (IMOC)

An incident management operations center should be established by the first agency to respond to an incident. Usually, that will be the Fire Department, and they will probably declare themselves incident commanders, which is fine, because the response is totally focused on lifesaving and property preservation. However, once the focus of the incident switches from lifesaving to decedent operations the management of the incident should begin by multiple agencies. Each primary agency should have a representative at the incident management operations center.

The incident management operations center should:

- Be staffed 24 hours a day

- Operate two 12-hour shifts initially, with a one-hour shift-change briefing
- Go to three 8-hour shifts, with a 30-minute shift-change briefing as the incident stabilizes
- Be in a restricted area
- Be located close to the incident site
- Be the location where all decisions are made
- Be a place where disagreements and concerns can be discussed privately

Law Enforcement Operations

A primary or lead law enforcement agency should be appointed to head up all law enforcement operations. Depending on the size of the incident and the resources of the primary law enforcement agency support law enforcement agencies should take responsibility for sub activities (Figure 1.2).

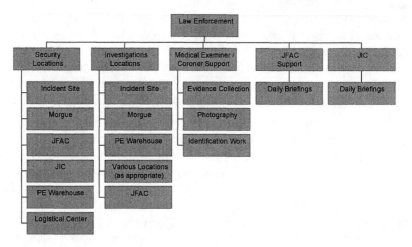

Figure 1.2 An organizational chart depicting the various law enforcement activities that may be required at a mass fatality incident. Note: JFAC—Joint Family Assistance Center; JIC—Joint Information Center; PE—Personal Effects.

Major Law Enforcement Activities:

- Security
- Investigations
- Medical Examiner and Coroner Support

Law Enforcement Sub Activities:

1. Security locations

- Incident site
- Mass fatality incident morgue
- Personal effects warehouse
- Joint family assistance center
- Joint information center
- Logistical support center

2. Investigations
   - Incident site
   - Mass fatality incident morgue
   - Personal effects warehouse
   - Various other locations, as appropriate

3. Medical Examiner and coroner support
   - Mass fatality incident morgue
   - Joint family assistance center
   - Various victim residences (as needed, to collect antemortem identification information and samples)

Joint Family Assistance Operations

A primary or lead agency should be appointed to head up all family assistance activities. In all incidents support will be required and should be used. In any one jurisdiction, usually any of several different agencies can act as the lead agency. I would consider using victim assistance departments, social services, and mental health departments. Strong consideration should also be given to appointing private organizations, if they are willing and able to participate, such as the local Red Cross or Salvation Army.

Family Assistance Major Activities

- Joint family assistance center
- Various locations, to meet with families, as appropriate

Decedent Operations (Figure 1.3)

Usually the ME is appointed the lead agency for all decedent operations. In some areas the medical examiner is part of a law enforcement operation. Depending on the size of the incident and the resources of the ME, supporting agencies should take responsibility for sub activities.

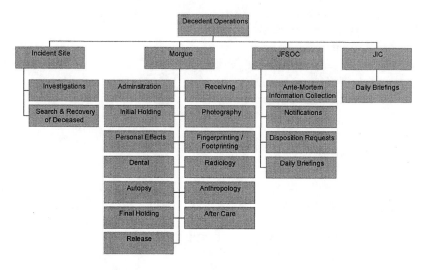

Figure 1.3 An organizational chart depicting the various decedent activities that may be required at a mass fatality incident.

Major Medical Examiner Activities

- Search and recovery of the deceased
- Medicolegal death investigation
- Ante-mortem information collection

Medical Examiner Sub Activities

1. Search and recovery of the deceased
   a. Incident site
   b. Movement to the mass fatality incident morgue

2. Medicolegal Death Investigation
   a. Incident site
   b. Mass fatality incident morgue
      - Administration
      - Receiving
      - Holding
      - Photography
      - Personal Effects
      - Fingerprinting or footprinting
      - Dental
      - Radiology
      - Autopsy and inspection

- Anthropology
- Final holding
- After Care
- Release

3. Ante-mortem Information Collection
   a. Joint family assistance center

Media Operations

A primary or lead agency should be appointed to head up all media activities. In all incidents every primary agency with a media specialist should provide that person to support media operations. The agency with the most experienced media spokesperson should take the role of the primary agency, however, only individual agency spokespersons should speak on behalf of a specific agency.

Major Media Activities

- Joint information center
- Incident site
- Logistics operations
- Incident management operations center

Personal Effects Operations (Figure 1.4)

Ideally, a private contractor or a law enforcement agency should be appointed to head up all personal effects operations. Depending on the number of personal effects recovered from the incident and the resources of the primary agencies, supporting law enforcement agencies may be required.

Major Personal Effects Activities

- Search and recovery of personal effects
- Personal effects warehouse
- Medical Examiner / Coroner Support

Personal Effects Sub Activities

1. Search and recovery of personal effects
   a. Incident site
   b. Movement to the personal effects warehouse

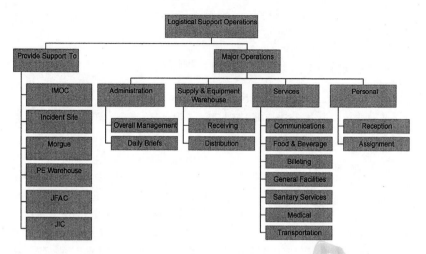

Figure 1.4 An organizational chart depicting the various personal effects activities that may be required at a mass fatality incident.

    c. Receipt from third parties or mass fatality incident morgue

2. Personal effects warehouse
   a. Administration
   b. Receiving operations
   c. Storage
   d. Processing
   e. Disposition
   f. Destruction

3. Medical Examiner or Coroner support
   a. Mass fatality incident morgue

Logistical Support Operations (Figure 1.5)

Not all incidents will require a separate logistical support operation. If the magnitude of the mass fatality incident is such that it requires the establishment of a logistical support operation, the agency not yet tasked should be picked as the primary agency. Depending on its resources, supporting agencies should also be assigned. I recommend agencies such as local supply and support departments, purchasing departments, or recreation departments.

Logistics support is provided to all areas. They are:

• Incident management operations center

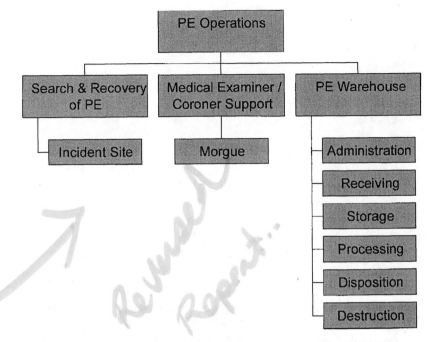

Figure 1.5 An organizational chart depicting the various logistical activities that may be required at a mass fatality incident.

- Incident site
- Mass fatality incident morgue
- Personal effects warehouse
- Joint family assistance center
- Joint information center
- Logistical support center

Major Logistical Support Activities

- Support administration
- Supply and equipment warehouse
- Services
- Personal

Logistical Support Sub Activities

- Support administration
  a. Logistical support operation

- Supply and equipment warehouse

    a. Receiving
    b. Distribution

  • **Services**
    a. Communications
    b. Food and beverage
    c. Billeting
    d. General facilities
    e. Sanitary services
    f. Medical
    g. Transportation

Finance and Administration Support

Not all incidents will require a separate finance and administration support operation. If the magnitude of the mass fatality incident is such that it requires the establishment of these support operations, an agency that has not yet been tasked should be picked as the primary agency. Depending on the resources of that agency, supporting agencies should also be assigned. I would recommend agencies such as local budget or personnel offices. The duties of this office should be to collect and track response expenses for the incident. This office should maintain oversight of spending activities. Even in incidents where a finance and administration support operation is not established, each responding agency should track and account for all spending to ensure all possible reimbursement can be recovered.

Summary

By definition, mass fatality incidents exceed the local jurisdiction's capabilities; in a sense, they are unmanageable. Taken as whole, the incident is unmanageable for one person or agency. Therefore, no one person or agency commands a mass fatality incident response. Many agencies will respond to an incident with different tasks and goals. In order to ensure a successful incident resolution, the agency leaders should meet to establish a response, and actions should then be implemented that enhance the completion of the group goals without sacrificing any one agency's responsibilities.

Organizing the response along functional lines makes the unmanageable manageable. Incidents in which a coordinated focused response was the management style have been those that have been remembered as model responses. On the other hand, incidents in which battle lines were drawn and response agencies acted without regard for other agencies, have been the impetus for changes in legislation and bitter memories for the families, responders, and communities.

Remember, there is no "I" in team. Work together and do a great job and there will be satisfaction for all; act independently without regard for the overall focus and few, if any, get satisfaction.

Incident Overview – A Quick Look

Initial Response Phases

To begin to understand how an incident is resolved one needs to look at the phases of response. Remember that we are dealing with known deceased and the response is no longer focused on life or property preservation. Responders must continue to remind themselves that too much speed in the initial response often results in the delay of release or the inability to accurately complete required governmental investigative reports.

This section focuses mainly on providing an outline of the medical examiner's operations flow. More detail is directed at the initial establishment of operations, as the other areas (establishment of the mass fatality morgue, search and recovery, personal effects, family assistance, and media operations) are covered more fully in other chapters.

Notification and Response Strategy Formulation (0–12 hrs.)

The primary focus in this, the initial phase of response, is to notify the ME of the incident. The ME must make several key decisions, based on his or her assessment of the situation, about the appropriate course of action to take.

Notification to the Medical Examiner

When the ME is notified that a mass fatality incident has occurred, notification should include the following:

- Type of incident

- Location
- Estimated number of fatalities
- Condition of bodies
- Demographics of those killed
- Ongoing response actions
- Response agencies currently on scene or en route

Medical Examiner Staff Notification

Once the medical examiner has been notified that an incident has occurred, notification and recall of key medical examiner staff should begin. Key staff includes:

- Office administrator
- Forensic pathologist
- Media spokesperson
- Logistics chief
- Chief investigator
- Senior morgue technician

These members may be a part of the full-time staff of the ME's office, or they may be part of another agency, in which case preexisting agreements should allow for their temporary assignment or day-to-day supervision to be transferred to the ME's office.

Medical Examiner Site Assessment

While the ME's staff is being notified and recalled, the ME should go to the incident site.
Once on scene, the ME should:

- Meet with the current incident commander and receive a status briefing.
- Observe the site.
- Observe the surrounding area.

Key questions and their importance to the ME are:

1. Is the incident stabilized, and if not, when it will be?

This will give the medical examiner an estimate of how long he has to establish operations. Many key decision factors will depend on the incident. For example, if it is an incident at sea, how long will it take for remains to start being brought to shore? If it is a building collapse, when will the building be safe to begin search and recovery operations? Will all remains be recovered at once or will the recovery be spread out over several days or weeks?

2. How many fatalities are there believed to be?

Although the number of deceased may not be the key issue, nonetheless it is important to know the number as this will give the ME an idea of how many ante-mortem identification records will be required, and how many families will need to be contacted.

3. What are the conditions of the bodies?

The ME should view several of the fatalities to get a picture of their condition. As mentioned earlier, there is perhaps no greater impact on guiding the overall response operations than the condition of the bodies.

Author's note: In any one incident the condition of the deceased can vary from viewable, intact remains to fragments no larger than a few ounces. In 1986, after an inflight shooting, a commercial aircraft plummeted from 10,000 feet, wreckage was scattered over a 50-acre area, and no portion of human remains greater than four pounds was recovered. Forty-nine people lost their lives in that incident.

4. Have the bodies been moved, and if so to where?

If a large number of bodies have been moved to a holding area, perhaps that area might be suitable for the establishment of a temporary morgue. Additionally, no other movement should occur until the ME has established the recovery parameters.

What the ME Should be Considering at this Time

1. Should a temporary morgue be established?

Key factors to consider are:

- The numbers of fatalities and their condition
- The distance from the incident site to an established morgue
- The availability of suitable facilities for the establishment of a temporary morgue
- Can the regular morgue accommodate and expand if needed for response to the incident
- What will be the impact on the permanent morgue's normal day-to-day caseload, and will the ME be able to keep the regular cases separate from the mass fatality incident cases

- If a temporary morgue is established, are necessary resources to equip it available

2. If a temporary morgue is to be established, where should it be located?

Key factors to consider are:

- Is there a suitable location close to the incident site?
- Does the facility support compliance with all OSHA regulations?
- Does it have controlled access, to keep the public and specifically photographers back, but still allow access for removal vehicles and responders?
- Does the facility have the basics—water, and sewer, electricity and climate control—or can they be supplied through the use of auxiliary support items?

3. What additional resources will be required, such as:

- Staff
- Equipment
- Funding
- What is the expected end state? (In other words, will it be an attempt at confirmed identification, and complete medicolegal autopsy or an attempt at establishing a confirmed identification with autopsy of a sampling and others as specified by law, such as the flight crew in a aircraft accident?)

4. What other response actions by other agencies might occur concurrently with ME operations?

Things to consider are the roles of other investigators who may want to examine the bodies to look for and collect evidence, may want to take possession of all personal effects, want specific tests conducted on the deceased to look for the presence of particular substances, or want you to conduct recoveries as they are still in the process of making the scene safe.

At this time, the medical examiner can remain on scene and direct the now-recalled staff to meet at a predetermined location or the ME can return to the office. I recommend that the ME remain on scene until the operation is established. This is to ensure that no damage or further damage to the scene occurs, that they can provide guidance to the current incident commander, and that they can direct and ensure that incident response follows protocol from the beginning.

The ME should take a few minutes with key staff and put into action the response plan based on the site assessment and the answering of key issues previously discussed. Hopefully, this will involve the adjustment of a preexisting plan, if not, try to follow as closely as possible the normal policies and procedures of your routine operations.

The ME should now establish key leaders who will then begin getting areas established and operating. The ME should not be placed in charge of specific areas; response is better managed when the leader can focus attention on the overall incident and quickly lift and shift direct focus to specific areas when needed.

Listed below are the key medical examiner operations and the positions I suggest should be responsible for supervising the operation. Some of these people may not be part of your regular staff, but to ensure a certain level of trust, you should have some prior experience with them and they with you.

- Morgue operations should be led and managed by the senior morgue administrator.

- Search and recovery operations should be led and managed by the senior death investigator.

- Family assistance operations should be led and managed by the senior victim coordinator or advocate.

- Media operations should be led and managed by the next-senior morgue administrator

- Logistical operations should be led and managed by the senior budget or supply and services person.

- Personal effects operations should be led and managed by the senior evidence technician.

Few ME offices have these people and positions as part of their regular staff. That's the challenge in a mass fatality incident; you simply have more deceased than you can handle using existing resources. Bring in help; look at what's available in your jurisdictional areas. For example, as suggested above, use the local victim services coordinator to act as your family assistance operations chief. Use your local supply and services person to be your "supply sergeant." By involving other agencies and tapping into their various specialties you will reduce the burden on your office and allow others to be part of the response, not to mention probably getting the right person for the right job.

Once these people have been assigned their positions, they should at once begin to establish their operations.

We have now looked at the points and possible courses of action for the medical examiner to consider and made some suggestions as to who should lead those operations. Now we will continue to look at the phases of response that begin after the ME has decided on a response strategy.

Establishment of Operational Areas (12–24 hrs.)

The primary focus in this stage of the ME's response is notification and recall of key personnel, site assessment, and the establishment of operations.

Specific actions:

- Lifesaving action continues.

- Search and recovery of deceased begins.

- Mass fatality incident morgue is established.

- Family assistance center is established.

- Local families begin to gather.

- Remains arrive at the mass fatality morgue or staging area.

- Response coordination briefings are conducted.

- Advance party of outside agencies (response support, compliance inspectors, and various investigators) begins to arrive.

- Logistical support operations are established.

All Operational Areas Up and Running (24–36 hrs.)

The primary focus in this stage of the medical examiner's response is search and recovery of the deceased, determining that all operations are fully functional, and overseeing the arrival of outside support agencies.

Specific actions:

- Search and recovery continues.

- Mass fatality morgue establishment continues (at this point many of the morgue stations are operational).

- Remains continue to arrive at the morgue.

- Media briefings are conducted.

- Family briefings are conducted.

- Families start to gather at the joint family assistance center. They are interviewed privately and detailed questionnaires about the missing are completed. These questionnaires will give detailed information such as a physical description about those presumed to be dead, names and addresses of dentists, doctors, and other primary caregivers who can provide preexisting records to aid in the identification.

- Families who do not come to the site are contacted. They can be interviewed by telephone, or their local ME or law enforcement can be asked to interview them. The same detailed questionnaires used at the joint family assistance center need to be completed.

- Main group of outside response agencies begins to arrive.

- Logistical operations continue.

Sustained Operations Search and Recovery—Morgue

(At this stage, it is difficult to establish a time line because each incident is so different.) The primary focus in this stage of the medical examiner's response is search and recovery of the deceased, their confirmed identification, the medicolegal autopsy, and the sustainment of all operational areas.

Specific actions:

- Search and recovery continues.

- Mass fatality morgue is fully operational.

- Remains continue to arrive at the morgue.

- Media briefings are continued.

- Family briefings are continued.

- Family interviews are continued.

- Identification records continue to arrive.

- Medicolegal autopsy begins.

- Identification of fatalities begins.

- Identification records continue to be created for those victims without preexisting records.

- Outside response agencies are fully operational.

- Personal effects operations are established.

Sustained Morgue Operations—Release of Deceased

The primary focus in this stage of the ME's response is winding down of search and recovery of the bodies, the increasing tempo of confirmed identifications of the deceased, the medicolegal autopsy, and the sustainment of all operational areas.

Specific actions:

- Search and recovery begins to wind down.

- Mass fatality morgue is fully operational.

- Deceased continue to arrive at the morgue.

- Media briefing continues.

- Families begin to deal with the medical examiner one-on-one and family assistance center operations begin winding down.

- Identification records continue to arrive.

- Identification of fatalities continues.

- Medicolegal autopsies continue.

- Outside response agencies continue support operations.

- Notifications to families of positive identifications begin.

- Families are asked to make disposition instructions.

- Deceased are released from the medical examiner.

- Personal effects operations continue.

Sustained Morgue Operations—Increased Numbers of Deceased Released

The primary focus in this stage of the medical examiner's response is the winding down or conclusion of dedicated search and recovery, the increasing tempo of confirmed identifications and release of the deceased, the increasing tempo in personal effects operations, the winding down of outside support operations, and the continued sustainment of ongoing operational areas.

Specific actions:

- Search and recovery continues winding down.

- Mass fatality morgue is fully operational.

- Remains continue to arrive at the morgue sporadically.

- Media briefings are continued.

- Individual and group family briefings are continued.

- Identification records continue to arrive.

- Identification of bodies continues.

- Medicolegal autopsies continue.

- Outside response agencies support operations close out.

- Notifications of positive identifications continue.

- Families are asked to make disposition instructions.

- Deceased are released from the medical examiner's office.

- Personal effects operations continue.

Final Release of Deceased and Cessation of Operations

The primary focus in this stage of the medical examiner's response to a mass fatality incident is the occasional receipt of remains, the resolving of the most difficult identifications, and the increased release of the deceased. Personal effects operations are in full swing. During this phase the medical examiner may decide to shut down a temporary mass fatality morgue and consolidate all operations at the regular morgue.

Specific actions:

- Search and recovery is closed out.

- Mass fatality morgue is winding down or has been closed and operations transferred to regular morgue.

- Media briefings are continued.

- Individual and group family briefings are continued.

- Identification of deceased continues.

- Notifications to families that their relatives have been positively identified continue.

- Families are asked to make disposition instructions.

- Deceased are released from the medical examiner's office.

- Personal effects operations continue.

Final Actions, Completion of Incident Report

Primary focus in this, the final stage of the medical examiner's response to a mass fatality incident is the completion of all identifications, final decisions about those who cannot be identified, the completion and closing of all case reports, and the final inspection of the incident site to ensure that all remains have been recovered.

Specific actions:

• Occasional media briefings are conducted.

• Identification of deceased is completed.

• Notifications to family members of positive identifications continue.

• Families are asked to make disposition instructions.

• Deceased are released from the medical examiner's office.

• Personal effects operations continue.

This is a simple overview of a response to a mass fatality incident. As you can see, the management of that response is anything but simple. Several separate complex actions that are affected by and have an effect on each other, must occur simultaneously.

Summary

Although each mass fatality incident is unique, most incidents follow a similar response sequence. In later chapters of this guide I offer much greater detail about the specific actions that should occur. However, all incident responders at the management level should have an idea about the overall sequence of events. Thus they will have better understanding and appreciation for other managers' roles and responsibilities.

Coping with the Response to Mass Fatalities

3

An unfortunate fact of life today is that we are exposed to an ever-increasing amount of violent death. People see it in their own communities, on the covers of magazines, on prime-time television. Some of it is make believe, some is all too real, and most of it is senseless. However, these deaths are sterile in the sense that viewers are isolated from actual sensory impressions beyond what some editor or photographer may choose to have them see. They may even see images of grieving families, but they don't have to talk to them and they can't see us. If it gets too uncomfortable, they can just turn the page or change the channel.

Professionals such as people in the fire service, law enforcement, medical services, and death investigators will, by the nature of their profession, be asked to deal with more death and become more intimately involved in the reality of the death. However, that exposure often occurs in gradual doses, and usually junior or new people are teamed with more-seasoned partners. Furthermore, when an incident occurs, a particular responder's involvement may last only a few minutes or perhaps as much as several hours a day for a few days. Rarely does it go beyond that. Then, as fast as the incident occurred, it is replaced by another.

Additionally, responders most likely won't be repeatedly reminded or asked about the incident. To the majority of the public, there is nothing special about this particular death. After all, people die every day. When responders go home at night, if they don't remark on the incident to their families, they probably won't be asked about it. The television news and local newspaper will quickly be filled with other events.

Not so with a mass fatality incident; death in a mass fatality incident is usually sudden, unexpected, violent, and indiscriminate and the numbers

29

involved are staggering. All at once, our senses are overloaded with sights, smells, and sounds that most of us, as responders, will never forget. For several days, weeks, and sometimes even a month we work, eat, have time off, and sleep with nothing but the mass fatality incident. When we open a paper, turn on the television, or talk to friends, the incident is always there.

Therein lies the challenge to those who manage and respond to mass fatality incidents. That is to prepare yourself and your responders to cope with an incident, to mitigate the impact during the incident, and finally, to follow up after the incident. Facing the requirement early on and developing a response strategy will help to ensure that as many of the responders as possible will return to a normal routine after an event.

What follows are the basic effects of exposure of mass fatality incidents, the coping strategies, and information on critical incident-stress-management programs.

Mature Death Attitude

A mature death attitude is defined as how well we understand the feelings or thoughts we have about our own and others' deaths. It is important for you to understand what the impact of your attitudes about death has on your ability to respond to and cope with a mass fatality incident. Those responders who are uncomfortable with the fact of their own mortality and that of others will be confronted with a great amount of physical proof of mortality at a mass fatality incident. If you have a problem accepting the basic fact of death, then you will most likely not accept the reality of the mass fatality incident. The results of this can range from complete denial of the incident to sudden overwhelming realization of the facts and the resulting inability to do anything but just sit and try to comprehend the magnitude of what has happened. In either case, your ability to function as an effective responder or the likelihood you will have a speedy return to a regular routine after the incident is doubtful.

What is Death?

How do you gauge your attitudes about death? To begin with, you should look at the four basic tenets about death and how you feel about them. The four generally accepted tenets are:

1. Death is the end of life.
For the purposes of this guide, it means the ceasing of all body activity and functions. Simply put, the ability to live, fulfill the promise of life, and experience the emotions of life are no longer there.

2. Death is irreversible.
Occasionally, if lifesaving measures are instituted immediately after death, it can be reversed. However, in most cases, it cannot. The reality of the incident is that it is not a bad dream, people don't "wake up."

3. Death comes to every living thing.
No fountain of youth or magic life extensions exist. Dying is a part of living.

4. Death is, for the most part, unpredictable.
This tenet, more than any other, often brings the most arguments. In some cases, death may be predicable. For example, people who have severe medical problems may be given a period of life expectancy that is, for the most part, fairly accurate. Then there are people who engage in high-risk behavior and can reasonably expect their lives to end at a somewhat predicable rate. But most people really do not know when or how they will die. Death could come in a vehicle accident, through an undiagnosed medical condition such as a ruptured aneurysm, in a natural disaster, or just simply being in the wrong place at the wrong time.

In continuing to assess your attitudes about death, you should also look at how you view your own mortality. The value in doing is to ensure that when and if you are exposed to a mass fatality incident, you will be able to cope with the common thoughts and observations that new responders have a tendency to make. They tend to put themselves in the victim's place and observe how easily it might have been them. While those thoughts are to some extent true, it was not you who was killed. It was, in fact, somebody else. And yes, it could be you next time, but nobody knows when the next time will occur, so to dwell on it is pointless and counterproductive to resolving the incident.

Attitudes About Death in Actions or Thoughts

It is important to examine your attitudes toward the bodies of the deceased. At all times, our treatment must be respectful and ethical. However, individual definitions of "respectful" and "ethical" may be based on many things such things as religious teachings, local customs, and our personal experiences. Ethical treatment is based on doing the right thing with the right motivation.

The challenge for mass fatality incident responders and managers is that we have different religious teachings, we come from places with different customs, and have different personal experiences. The same applies to the families of the deceased. The solution to this challenge is do and remember a few basics.

- The end goal is returning the right remains to the right family. There is no higher ethical goal or respectful treatment then to ensure that families have the ability to make personal decisions about their family members or friends. Because of this, medicolegal autopsies may be performed and remains may be held by the ME for an extended period of time to ensure recovery of all parts of the remains.
- Remains will be covered and protected from public view at all times. Because of the need for controlled recovery or the nature of the incident, remains may be left at the incident site for a short while; if they are visible, they should be covered. The general public and media should not have access to a site until all remains have been recovered.
- Remains are treated in the same manner as we treat the living. Simple things such as properly carrying, picking up, and placing the bodies or fragments on gurneys and X-ray tables, etc., demonstrate the respect that they deserve. These are all very simple things, but regrettably are at times forgotten — usually by responders who have not accepted that the remains represent human life.

Treat the families with compassion and understanding; explain to them what you doing and why you are doing it. If they understand that your motivations are geared toward doing the right thing, most of them will support the actions.

Remember that what you are dealing with was once a human being. When discussing actions, formulating plans, and talking with families, press, and the general public, remember you are referring to bodies or body parts. Be careful in your terminology — referring to the mass fatality morgue as operating on an "assembly-line format" would be insensitive. Remains are not items to be run down an assembly line.

In addition to the benefits of knowing that you are doing what is ethically correct is the fact the public is watching you. The overall management of the incident will not be remembered for long, but your attitude toward the victims and their families will be remembered forever.

Effects On Responders

Responders and managers can be better prepared for the effects of the mass fatality incident stress if they must first understand the types of stress. Furthermore, I believe no matter how experienced a responder is; we all have our limits. When we reach those limits, it's neither good or bad, just reality.

A study conducted for the Emergency Planning Centre Canada, (Study on The Psychological Effects of Disaster On Operational Personnel, by Dr. Hélène Lamontagne, 1983) stated that, "Our work in emergency medicine over the last seven years led me to believe that the workers in emergency crews of all kinds, who went to the scene of a disaster, were profoundly affected by it, both while they were working there and in the following days/months."

Dr. Lamontagne made that statement some years ago. We have learned since then that the response to a mass fatality incident, if properly managed, can be structured to be less devastating to the responders. However, even with proper management, some responders will be so seriously affected by the experience that they will not be willing or able to return to work as responders.

Stress Effects

The following are the most common effects observed in mass fatality incident responders during and after incident response. How frequently they occur and their duration is dependent upon the responder and the mitigation program, if any, participated in. Some of these problems are similar to those outlined in Post Traumatic Stress Disorder (PTSD) cases. They are in addition to the normally expected physiological changes to the body.

Invasive images.   Mental pictures of the deceased or incident that come back to the responder's memory at inappropriate times.

Invasive smells.   Those smells that are common at a mass fatality incident. New responders who work directly with or have duties in the mass fatality morgue often report "smelling the incident" long after their role in the incident is over. Additionally, months later, something they smell that is totally unrelated may trigger a memory of the incident.

Being overwhelmed.   A sense of being completely overwhelmed, task saturated, or helpless can occur at both the management and responder level. It happens when a person feels that an incident is unmanageable and nothing they do will help. This is especially at the beginning of an incident, when the numbers of remains never seem to end.

Difficulty sleeping.   Many responders will, despite total exhaustion, have some trouble falling asleep. Once they do, they will often experience nightmares or invasive images. Others will go to great lengths to avoid going to sleep and the coming of night will be faced with trepidation

Strained Personal Relationships

It will come as no surprise to many that the divorce and relationship failure rate among professional responders (fire, police, and death investigator) is often very high.

Clearly it is difficult for people who have been involved in a mass fatality incident to be able to shut off that aspect of their lives and fall into the role of parents, spouses, or friends when they arrive home. It is also difficult for them to remember that the day-to-day activities that occur at home and in other people's lives are just as important to them as involvement in a mass fatality incident is to you.

In addition to the basic and somewhat common effects mentioned above, the special circumstances listed below may produce unique and unexpected problems, even for the most experienced responders.

Special Circumstances

These terms were first used in the landmark text *Individual and Community Responses to Trauma and Disaster: The Structure of Human Chaos,* (Robert J. Ursano, Brian G. McCaughey, and Carol S. Fullerton, Eds., Cambridge University Press, Cambridge, U.K., 1994.) However, the definitions are those of this author and may not completely correlate with those suggested by Drs. Ursano and McCarroll. Their definitions were based on interviews and studies of responders; mine are my own observations as an incident responder, incident manager, and military mortuary affairs company commander.

Children

When dispatched to a call involving a child, the fireman, policeman, or medic answering the call tends to move just a little bit faster. Emotions will run a little bit higher and people will take more risks. The same thing happens when children are victims in a mass fatality incident. Usual responses include greater anger and dismay.

Managers and responders must face the fact that children will possibly be among the victims. Responders who are unsure of themselves, or are tired and overworked may "break" when asked to work with children's remains

Author's note: During an incident in which several young children had been brutally murdered, the last missing child was brought to the temporary morgue. The staff who had been on duty for an extended period of time had to leave the morgue; they were simply overwhelmed. As I was finishing up the required actions, my wife called and had my young daughter, who was approximately the same age as the victim, start to talk to me. It is the only time I have ever not been able to continue with a conversation and been forced to stop what

I was doing. This was simply because the victim had been a child just like mine, but was now deceased.

Natural Looking

When a person responds to a mass fatality incident and discovers a body that shows little damage lying among significant wreckage and physical destruction, it can be difficult for a responder to accept the fact that with so little trauma a person could have been killed in the incident. Although it is not usual to find victims of building collapses or transportation accidents fairly intact, it is not unheard of.

When responders come upon such remains, they may begin to question whether the person is really dead, or perhaps even think it is a cruel joke.

Sensory Stimuli

In cases where the remains could not be recovered for some time, if the weather was conducive to rapid decomposition, and if odorous chemical agents (such as aviation fuels) are present, the senses of the responder can be overwhelmed. Add to this the feel of the remains when they are recovered, and during the established response protocol the combination can produce profound stimulation.

On the other hand, in cases where encapsulating personal protective devices are used, responders may feel very isolated and cut off from other responders, as they have a lack of sensory stimuli.

Novelty, Surprise, Shock

Any one of these reactions occurs when we are confronted with something that is confusing to our normal senses — even the incident scene itself. For example, any responder who has been to an aviation accident in a residential area may recall the disbelief in looking a large part of an aircraft protruding though the roof of a house. It just is not a normal sight and the two major objects combined in that context do not make sense to our minds. The same thing happens when responders see bodies that may be grossly disarticulated, damaged, or missing major portions.

Watch what happens when a body is brought into a mass fatality incident morgue. Less-experienced individuals will stand back, they will make conclusions about what to expect based on the condition of previously recovered remains, on what they have heard the more experienced responders describe and on the condition of the human-remains pouch (body bag). Yet none of this may prepare them for what they actually see. The remains could be a natural-looking child, or one that at first appears not to have much trauma, but as the pouch is further opened is, in fact, severely damaged.

Identification and Emotional Involvement

Some responders may become so involved in an incident that they develop a relationship with the deceased. They are the ones who will make statements that it could have easily been them or will wonder aloud what the surviving families will do after the loss of a loved one.

Certainly it is good for responders to be concerned about the families. I still maintain and enjoy contact with the family members of mass fatality incident victims. These contacts have enriched my life and serve to remind me the value of what I do. However, that is after the incident. During the incident response, the focus should be on maintaining a nonemotional involvement. In incidents where responders stand a good chance of knowing and recognizing a victim, such as in smaller communities, or an accident, or attack on a government building, managers must be especially aware of responders and themselves identifying with the victims and /or becoming emotionally involved.

Personal Effects

The challenges of working with mass fatality incident victims' personal effects are multiple and different from those faced by the responder working only with remains. Personal effects add a life and story to remains. Think about everything you carry with you, especially when you are most likely to be involved in a mass fatality incident, such as while traveling or at work. Most people have jewelry with inscriptions from loved ones, photographs of family, love letters and notes, toys for kids, personal journals, and many other similar things. All of these items serve to remind the responder of the impact of the incident.

Additionally, effecting the disposition of personal effects will undoubtedly take a long time, in average cases, a few years. Again, this can force the responder as well as the families to continually relive the incident.

Effects on Communities

In addition to the effects mass fatality incidents have on the incident responders and managers are the effects the incidents have on the community in which the incident occurs. These effects range from emotional impacts on the people to economical benefits and costs to community businesses.

"Community" in this sense may also be taken to mean a company or group who plays a large part in the incident. In other words, consider a small credit union located in a building that is destroyed by a bomb. Perhaps only a small portion of the staff survives. That bombing will have an impact on that "community" every day those who survived go to work in their new building — if in fact they can return to work at all. They will undoubtedly remember their lost co-workers.

In another example, take an aviation incident. Whatever the cause of the incident, the airline as a community will suffer. Ticket agents who sold the tickets, mechanics who serviced the plane and others involved with the flight may suffer greatly. Not only will they have also lost friends and co-workers, they will surely question what role — if any — they played in the incident.

Emotional Impact

The type of incident and the community in which the incident occurs will have a great bearing on the emotional impact. The smaller and closer-knit a community is, the greater the impact. Additionally, communities located away from the incident may also be affected. In this age of affordable travel many schools and community groups travel great distances. When the craft in which they are traveling crashes with a large loss of life, the home community will also be impacted.

How that impact affects certain groups depends on the group itself. Just as each incident is different so is the impact it has on different groups of people.

Adults

Generally, adults in a community will react with disbelief, anger, and shock. After the realization of the incident sets in, they will react in different ways. Many will want to help and provide whatever support they can. Some will want to come to the site, take pictures and just look, some will go even further and try to access the site to get souvenirs. And yet some will take action by organizing recovery activities and support groups. Some may even draft and propose legislation to enhance or improve future response actions.

Today, in the United States alone, there are several groups that have been formed in direct response to mass fatality incidents and other disasters. Groups such as the National Foundation for Mortuary Care and National Disaster Medical Systems Disaster Mortuary Teams were a direct result of people realizing that there had to be a better way to respond.

Children

Children react to mass fatality incidents differently from the way adults do, because they don't understand the concept of death. They also don't comprehend the magnitude of a mass fatality incident. They do, however, sense when the adults are afraid. Since adults also react emotionally, children may become terrified. If the incident was one in which children were the majority of the victims or even the target, such as in a school shooting, the impact will be even greater.

The challenge for the community then becomes how to alleviate these fears and help the children recover and resume a sense of normalcy. Even when, to an adult, there is no basis for fear, to a child, imagined danger can seem as threatening as real danger.

Economical Impact

As we have thus far seen, mass fatality incidents impact the responders and various communities in many ways. One way is in impact to the economy. This can have both negative and positive aspects.

Negative Impacts

Negative impacts might include the decline or closure of a business. Some transportation companies have seen their revenue plummet or have gone out of business following incidents for which they had very little culpability. One must remember that a business is composed of many workers, not just the owners or stockholders. Other impacts are a possible loss of revenue as a result of "bad publicity" surrounding the incident. Many small businesses may be forced to close forever simply because they lost personnel, equipment, and facilities in the incident.

Positive Impacts

Positive impacts include an increase in business for people and businesses that provide logistical support to incoming responders, family members, and media personnel. Industries such as lodging, rental vehicle companies, eating establishments, and suppliers will be in demand following an incident. It is also important to note that these "positives" are temporary in that these same industries may suffer later from the notoriety of the incident. Additionally, they may have to turn away long-time patrons to provide facilities and support to the incoming responders, families, and media personnel.

It is also important to note that, in my personal experience, no support industry has ever provided less than an outstanding level of support and often at a fair or even below market price. It is a true statement to say that after such horrible events, the best in people often comes out.

Legislation

One of the greatest impacts of mass fatality incidents has been the introduction, and in some cases rapid approval, of legislation in direct response to a mass fatality incident. The focus and manner of legislation compliance has also changed. For example, after several significant major air crashes, the Federal Aviation Family Assistance Act of 1996 was introduced, passed, and signed into public law very rapidly. Its total focus is on response and preparing for response. It codifies and tasks many different agencies with specific actions designed to help the families, and impacted responding jurisdictions. It also has punitive measures for anyone who violates or impedes the response of certain agencies.

On the other hand, in the 1980s, after one year of several deadly hotel fires, some deliberate and others accidental, the Hotel and Motel Safety Act was passed. It focused only on prevention, ensuring that hotels and motels installed sprinkler systems, safety doors, and other fire-suppression methods. It had no punishments, but merely sought compliance by prohibiting federal government lodging contracts to those establishments that did not meet the Act's requirements.

The down side to this legislation, which I have termed "emotional legislation," because it is often introduced, passed, and signed into public law following a series of incidents, is that at times it is based on emotion and not a full understanding of the various response systems. For example, the Federal Aviation Family Assistance Act of 1996 was done with no or little input from the medical examiner's perspective, yet it has a major impact on the ME during an aviation incident.

We have now spent some time talking about who is affected and how they are affected by responding to a mass fatality incident. Following are some coping strategies that may help mitigate or lessen the impact of the response.

Stress Mitigation Programs

A large part of the success or failure of a person to adequately handle the stress of involvement in a mass fatality incident is their willingness to actively participate in a mitigation program. But first, their agency must recognize and support the need for a structured stress mitigation program.

There are three stages of coping:

1. Actions taken before an incident occurs
2. Actions accomplished during an incident
3. Actions taken after an incident

Throughout all the phases two things are essential. One is that individual reactions and abilities vary in the different stages of response and, to a larger degree, with the level and sophistication of responder experience. The other essential item is supervisor and peer support. The leaders and a majority of your peers must support the stress mitigation programs. As you will see, they play a key role in the program.

The goal of these stress mitigation programs is to have every responder return from an incident intact, both physically and mentally.

Coping Before

This phase of the stress mitigation program is an agency responsibility. It involves several key areas.

• Practice Drills

By participating in tough, realistic training exercises, responders will have an idea of what to expect. This should greatly reduce the anxiety and stress experienced by those who do not know what to expect.

• Briefings or Classes

Bring in experts on critical incident stress, which we will talk about in the next section. Bring in responders who have been through a real incident and have them talk about their own experiences — what they thought about, what physical changes they experienced during and after an incident. Having experienced responders describe going through an incident and surviving it reinforces the understanding that, although a lot of things that happen may be unpleasant, eventually they go away and most things return to normal.

• Family Involvement

Do not forget to involve the responders' family members. They should be invited to participate in classes and training events. During these events they should learn about changes and differences in behavior their spouses may exhibit when involved in a mass fatality incident. Some people may discover that incident response is something they or their families are unwilling or unable to participate in. Nothing is wrong with that, and it is obviously better to have that information up front.

• Physical Fitness

The benefits of being physically fit have been well established. People who exercise regularly and maintain an appropriate weight are less prone to stress-induced health problems and work-related injuries. Unfortunately, the majority of people who respond to mass fatality incidents do not regularly participate in exercise programs. Being in good condition will play enormous dividends when you must draw upon everything you have in the first few hours and days of an incident.

Coping During

In this phase, voluntary participation is stressed, but mandatory participation may be warranted for some responders. However, the success of the program will depend on an individual's willingness to participate. In this phase, all actions are conducted on or near the incident site.

- **Know Your Staff**

Sounds simple enough, but the key will be to take the time necessary to look at the people you supervise or your peers and see how well they are holding up. Sometimes a simple shift in work assignment or an encouraging remark such as, "I know how you're feeling," "Don't worry about it, it's natural," or "You're doing a good job," is all it takes.

I have found that scheduling an evening stand-up or staff meeting, regardless of how busy I am allows me the time to hear and see my responders. Additionally, taking time for one-on-one conversations with a different responder every day will give you a feel for how things are going. People are much more willing to talk and express their true feelings one-on-one. I cannot overemphasize the importance of this. Know your people and listen to what they say, and observe what they do.

- **Professional Staff Support**

Have a trained professional mental-health provider on staff. This person should move around the site, mingle with and talk with responders. The more they get to know and win the confidence of the responders, the better job they will be able to do.

I caution against having too many mental-health providers. Some people may really not need that much attention, but if told enough times that they should have, they might develop problems where none existed or where they were manageable before.

- **Briefings**

No matter how experienced your personnel are, all incoming responders should be briefed about what to expect at the incident they are responding to. They should be told if there are children involved, the numbers and conditions of the deceased, and the condition of the incident site. If basic operational methods have changed or people are coming from outside your jurisdiction or agency they should be introduced to key leaders and told how your agency operates.

- **Gradual Exposure**

If at all possible, you should strive to expose inexperienced responders to the realities of a mass fatality incident gradually and in a controlled manner. This can be done by controlling what areas they work in and for how long they work at a particular area. For example, the first day, they may work in the administrative section of the morgue or be assigned to search an area on the periphery of an incident site.

- **Human Needs**

Ensuring those basic human needs such as sleep, food and beverages, facilities for personal hygiene, and time off are an important part of ensuring stress management. The general tendency will be for responders to forget about themselves and to keep going until they collapse. The problem with that is threefold.

1. You very quickly run out of responders, especially senior leaders, who seem to be the worst at taking care of themselves.

2. As you wear down, you become more susceptible to stress-related problems.

3. Your judgment tends to suffer and you make more mistakes.

Responders should not work at an incident indefinitely; every 4 or 5 days they should have some time away from the site. It does not have to be an entire day, but of course, that is preferable.

- **Pairing with Experienced Personnel**

When you have several inexperienced people, an effective stress-mitigation program is to pair them up with senior, more-experienced personnel. A note of caution: Ensure that the senior person is willing to work with, teach, mentor, and guide a new person. One of the worst things you can do is place an inexperienced individual with someone who would be just as happy to see them fail as to see them succeed. This goes back to knowing your people.

- **Interaction and Humor**

It has long been known that peer support and a sense of humor will go a long way to help ease the stress of response. Sometimes, the humor is not understood by non-responders and it is often called gallows humor, but, for the most part, it is not disrespectful. No responder ever stands alone; those who do often find themselves alienated and do not last. Mass fatality incident response is a team response. Success depends on your ability to get along and take the situation — but not yourself — seriously.

Coping After

This phase is often the most neglected or completely forgotten phase, and it can be the most important one. It is easy to see why it often goes by the wayside. During an incident, the focus is on the incident and the incident response, but later, most people want to forget about it, whether they were involved or not. New things become important, other work comes up, priorities get adjusted. Some responders will cope quite well without after care, but what about the ones who don't? If a structured after-care program is not in place, they may "fall through the safety net." At a minimum, they will most likely never recover from the incident and will, for all intents and purposes, become another victim or, in the worst-case scenario, commit suicide. This phase may last weeks or even months, depending on the magnitude and scope of the incident.

Family and Organizational Involvement

Shortly after an incident, responders' families should be offered an opportunity to participate in scheduled debriefings led by a mental-health professional. Family members should be allowed to ask questions and express any feelings. They should also be provided with information about the anticipated timeline the responders might be expected to return to pretty much routine lifestyle.

It is also a good idea for responders and their families to get together in a social context. This allows people to observe each other and see how everyone is doing. People having trouble may not be comfortable asking for help directly, but may exhibit signs to a peer who was involved in the incident with them, but who may not have seen them or worked with them since the mass fatality incident.

• Recognition and Awards

Unfortunately, some people participate in a mass fatality incident response for the public recognition and awards given to them. Fortunately, the majority of responders do it because they know that it is job that needs to be done and it requires people with special skills and motivation. Nonetheless, it is gratifying and important for all individuals to know that the part they played in an incident response was indeed valuable and significant to the overall recovery effort.

Therefore, when the incident response starts to wind down, but while the majority of responders are still present, a recognition ceremony where some type of small award or token of recognition is presented and responders are publicly thanked should occur. If possible, local politicians or other community leaders should speak and also thank the responders for their involvement in bringing resolution to the incident.

- **Critical Incident Stress Debriefing**

Critical Incident Stress Management was a term first used by Dr. Jeffrey T. Mitchell in 1986; the term has been used widely and is sometimes called Critical Incident Stress Debriefing (CISD). CISD is a structured program best conducted by trained mental-health professionals and peer counselors. Its usefulness and effectiveness have been well documented and supported. Various studies comparing the number of responders who return to regular habits and activities after incidents is significantly higher among agencies who follow and use a CISD program as opposed to those agencies who do little or nothing.

The goal of a CISD program is to mitigate the impact and speed recovery. It is a three-part program that differs from the actions taken during an incident in that it is designed as an exit program for those responders ending their involvement in the incident.

Phase 1: Debriefing

This phase is conducted on or near the incident scene. It is somewhat informal, and should happen before responders leave the incident scene or surrounding area. In this phase, an experienced, but non-incident-involved mental-health professional or peer counselor will talk with the responders. Responders should feel free to say anything and express any feelings. Responders should also be told what later reactions to expect and that those things are natural and experienced by most people who respond to mass fatality incidents. They should be also told not to be critical of each other or to question their own actions but to remember the value of what they have accomplished and the role they played.

This phase should be mandatory. If for any reason whatsoever a responder cannot attend this debriefing, written points of contact and basic information sheets describing the anticipated effects of incident response should be provided to everyone who was involved in the incident response.

Phase 2: Formal Program

This phase of the program should occur three days after incident responders have completed their involvement in incident response. It is led by a CISD team, which should include both mental-health professionals and peer counselors. It should also be mandatory for all responders involved in the incident. Some basics: People do not have talk or say anything if they don't want to, no one should take notes, statements made stay in the CISD program and should not be used as a means for termination or personnel action, and care should be taken not to criticize incident management. Certainly those comments and purposeful criticism have their place, but that is not in stress mitigation programs. The simple reasoning behind this is so that no one is put on the defensive.

The six parts of this formal program are

a. **Introduction:** Sets the ground rules, and responders introduce themselves.

b. **Facts:** Sets the facts of the incident and reviews incident specifics.

c. **Thoughts:** Responders talk about the first thoughts they had on arrival at the incident and beginning work.

d. **Feelings and symptoms:** Responders talk about what their overall reaction to the incident is, what are they feeling now, and what unusual things have happened to them, such as invasive images or smells.

e. **Teaching:** The CISD Team reassures responders that what they are feeling and experiencing is to be expected and that they will survive. Additionally, they should provide specific stress-response methods based on the dynamics of the group. Different groups of responders will have different needs.

f. **Reentry:** In this, the final part of Phase 2, responders should ask any final questions. Those responders who appear to need additional assistance should be referred to more-intense one-on-one help. The session should conclude with a wrap-up or summary by the CISD team leader.

Phase 3: Follow up

The last after strategy is simply to follow up on responders who may be having difficulty readjusting to a regular routine even after all other programs have ended. In these cases, the complete care should be turned over to professional mental-health workers who can recommend an appropriate course of action and treatment. Usually, there are not many in any one supervisor's care or peer circle who are having difficulty adjusting, but the point here is not to forget about those few.

Summary

The ability to respond to a mass fatality incident and mitigate the normal stresses associated with your involvement in that incident will depend on several key factors. Those factors include whether you have a mature attitude toward death, the coping mechanisms in place before, during, and after an incident, and how willingly you participate in those programs.

If you are a supervisor, it is all the more important to ensure that you know your people and take charge of ensuring their good mental health, know their warning signs, and intervene before damage is done. Finally, don't forget those people who were involved but easily forgotten because they played a minor role.

Responder Protection

4

During a mass fatality incident response, responders may be exposed to biological hazards in the form of contact with blood, body fluids, and unfixed tissue or organs. At the same time, they may also be exposed to hazardous materials in the form of such things as various fuels used by the transportation industry, asbestos used in building construction, various chemicals released by cargo carriers involved in transportation accidents, and chemical agents used in morgue operations.

Not only do incident managers have a moral responsibility to provide safeguards, they also have a legal responsibility. However, that leader responsibility does not negate the individual responsibility to use the protective equipment provided (see Figure 4.1), common sense, and to follow the instructions provided.

Furthermore, it is not unusual—in fact, it is to be expected—that compliance inspectors will arrive fairly rapidly at a mass fatality incident scene to ensure adherence to the various laws.

This chapter will discuss the U.S. legal requirements and provide some practical methods to ensure compliance and safety during incident response. We will also cover another area of responder protection; that is, from lawsuits for actions taken during a mass fatality incident.*

Federal Requirements—Biological Hazards

The Occupational Health and Safety Administration (OSHA) has mandated that its standards apply to all private-sector employees with one or more

---

* The information provided here refers to the resolution of "routine" mass fatality incidents; no attempt is made to discuss the additional requirements when dealing with and focusing on response to an event involving an accidental or intentional release of a chemical, biological, or nuclear agent. Procedures for these incidents do exist, but they are too lengthy to present here.

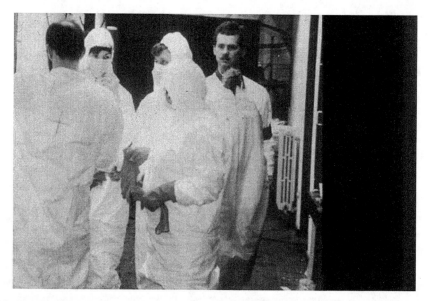

Figure 4.1   Mass fatality incident morgue workers dressed in appropriate personal protective equipment for exposure to bloodborne pathogens. Please note the Tyvek suits, gloves, and face masks. (Courtesy of Kenyon International Emergency Services, Inc.)

employees, as well as federal civilian employers. States administering their own occupational safety and health programs through various laws must adopt standards and enforce requirements that are at least as effective as federal requirements. The standards specified are codified under Part 1910.1030 of Title 29 of the Code of Federal Regulations. They became effective March 6, 1992.

For those readers not subject to OSHA guidelines, I strongly encourage your adoption or use of similar standards; they work for your protection.

Components of a response strategy and requirements of the law include:

* Defining who is covered by the standard.

* What the threat is.

* Creating and using an exposure-control plan, which includes:
  a. Communicating the hazards to employees

  b. Defining what the preventive and control measures are

  c. What actions to take in the event of exposure

  d. Recordkeeping

Who is Covered

This determination must be made without regard to the protective clothing and equipment provided. During a mass fatality incident response, one would reasonably expect that individuals conducting any operations at the incident site are exposed, additionally, responders who specifically search for, recover, and work with remains, and responders who search for, recover, and work with personal effects might also be exposed.

The Threat

Responders should have protection that prevents parenteral, mucous-membrane, and non-intact skin exposures to blood or other potentially infectious materials. Infectious materials include:

- Visibly bloody fluid
- Semen
- Vaginal secretions
- Unfixed tissue or organs
- Cerebrospinal fluid
- Synovial fluid
- Pleural fluid
- Peritoneal fluid
- Pericardial fluid
- Amniotic fluid

Since the condition of the majority of remains at a mass fatality incident site is likely to be one of trauma, all fluids and any and all portions of remains should be considered potentially infectious carriers.

Written Exposure-Control Plan

Agencies must develop a written exposure-control plan to include who is at risk, by job classification or by specific task if completed by only some employees; the procedures for evaluating the circumstances surrounding an exposure incident; the schedule; method for implementing such compliance sections as hepatitis B vaccination; post-exposure follow-up; communication of hazards to employees; and recordkeeping.

For mass fatality incident response, I recommend that each agency maintain its own written exposure-control plan. When people from different agencies are integrated into another agency's operation, preexisting agreements should establish that the responsibility for training, hazard communication, and vaccinations will remain the responsibility of the agency providing the responder. In those cases when the providing agency does not have a viable plan in place, the receiving agency should provide a quick training plan, vaccinations, and the required notification forms to ensure their compliance with the law. Follow-up should then be the responsibility of the providing agency.

This again demonstrates the importance of having complete pre-incident coordinated plans.

Communicating Hazards To Employees

Each occupationally exposed employee must be given information and training. This training cannot be at any cost to the employee and must be provided at the time of initial assignment and at least once a year thereafter. Additional training is required when existing tasks are modified or new tasks are added.

Information includes:

- How to obtain a copy of the regulatory text and an explanation of its contents
- Information on the epidemiology and symptoms of bloodborne diseases
- Ways in which bloodborne pathogens are transmitted
- Explanation of the exposure-control plan and how to obtain a copy of it
- Information on how to recognize tasks that might result in occupational exposure
- Explanation of the use and limitations of works practices, engineering controls, and personal protective equipment
- Information on the types, selection, proper use, location, removal, handling, decontamination, and disposal of personal protective equipment
- Information on hepatitis B vaccination
- Information on who to contact and what to do in an emergency
- Information on how to report an exposure incident and on the post-exposure evaluation and follow-up
- Information on warning labels, signs, where applicable, and color coding
- Question-and-answer session on any aspect of training

The training must be conducted by a person who is knowledgeable about the subject and the information provided must be at the appropriate level (vocabulary, educational level, and content) for the participants.

Preventive Measures

1. Hepatitis B Vaccination

Agencies must make the hepatitis B vaccine and vaccination series available to all employees who have occupational exposure as well as provide a post-exposure evaluation and follow-up to all employees who experience an exposure incident. This must be provided at no cost to the employee.

Employees who decline the vaccination must sign a declination form and may request and obtain the vaccination at a later date, again at no cost to them, if they continue to be exposed.

The vaccine and vaccination series must be offered within 10 working days of initial assignment to employees who have occupational exposure to blood or other potentially infectious material as defined earlier in this chapter, unless:

- The employee has previously received the complete hepatitis B vaccination series.
- Antibody testing reveals that the employee is immune.
- Medical reasons prevent taking the vaccinations.

2. Universal Precautions

Standard universal precautions must be observed. This requires the agency and employee to assume that all human blood and specified body fluids are infectious for bloodborne pathogens. When it is difficult or impossible, such as in a mass fatality incident, to differentiate between types of body fluids, all body fluids should be considered potentially infectious.

Methods of Control

Various methods to protect responders and facilities against contamination exist, however, because mass fatality incidents rarely occur in locations in which established morgue facilities can be used, some creativity and thought must go into establishing and enforcing proper practices (Figure 4.2).

It is also at this point that leaders and peer involvement become critical. Setting the example and enforcing standards are the best things leaders and individual responders can do to ensure compliance.

Engineering Controls

Reduce responder exposure by either removing or isolating the hazard. In a mass fatality incident those controls include the use of Sharpes Containers, proper ventilation devices, use of plastic floor and wall coverings to allow for washing and decontamination, and use of nonporous material for work conducted around the remains and personal effects.

Figure 4.2   Mass fatality incident morgue workers dressed for protection against both bloodborne pathogens and exposure to hazardous materials (formaldehyde). (Courtesy of Kenyon International Emergency Services, Inc.)

Work Practice Controls

Work practice controls consist of establishing and enforcing specific requirements about the way the work is done. In a mass fatality incident those controls may include:

- Establishing a break area away from the morgue for eating and drinking
- Prohibiting smoking, application of cosmetics or lip balm in the morgue area (the goal here is the same as everywhere else, and that is to keep potentially contaminated hands away from the mouth, nose, and eyes)
- Establishing multiple handwashing stations

Personal Protective Equipment (PPE)

The use of PPE is also commonly referred to as part of using universal precautions. PPE is readily available, and although not inexpensive, it is cheap when the protection it provides is compared with the cost of failing to provide protection if an exposure and infection occurs or an agency is fined for failing to follow the law.

Personal protective equipment must be used if occupational exposure is still present after instituting engineering and work practice controls, or if these controls are not feasible.

Agencies must provide, make accessible, and require the use of PPE. Responders may temporarily and briefly decline to wear personal protective equipment under rare and extraordinary circumstances. This almost always applies to certain life-saving activities. I have yet to see it apply to a mass fatality incident. Agencies are also required to ensure that the PPE is being properly used and disposed of.

Personal Protective Equipment includes the following.

Gloves. Different responders will require different gloves; some may require two pairs of gloves at the same time. For example, responders recovering remains from wreckage may need to wear rubber gloves underneath work gloves; the work gloves will most likely need to be destroyed as contaminated waste.

Gowns. Just as with gloves, different responders will require different gowns. For some, paper/cloth types are sufficient, for others rubber or heavy material may be required.

Masks. Generally paper or cloth types of masks are sufficient, as long as they cover both the mouth and nose. However, the masks provide very little protection against odor (typically cadaverine, butyl mercaptide, and hydrogen sulfide, among others). In cases of extreme putrefaction, responders may want to consider using masks specifically designed as anti-putrefaction, such as those available through SIRCHIE Finger Print Laboratories, Inc.

Protective eyewear. Many different types of protective eyewear are available. They range from safety glasses or plastic shields attached to masks to full face shields. In this case, the level of protection needed will depend on the work environment.

Note: depending on your agency's need, there are many suppliers of protective barrier kits or individual products. I have used and recommend a Johnson and Johnson product called Barrier Kits,™ which contain gloves, face shields, gowns, biohazard bags, and hair coverings.

Housekeeping

Under this standard, each work area must be kept clean and sanitary. Quite obviously this will be a greater challenge during a mass fatality incident. Therefore, this factor is of great importance when making the decision about when and where to establish a mass fatality incident morgue. The simplest and easiest way to ensure that the mass fatality morgue can be cleaned is to use plastic covering that can be easily decontaminated or replaced.

Additionally, the following procedures must be followed.

- Decontaminate work surfaces with an appropriate disinfectant after completion of procedures, immediately when overtly contaminated, after any spill of blood or other potentially infectious materials, and at the end of the work shift when surfaces have been contaminated since the last cleaning.
- Remove and replace protective coverings such as plastic wrap and aluminum foil when contaminated.
- Inspect and decontaminate, on a regular basis, reusable receptacles such as bins, pails, and cans that might possibly become contaminated. When contamination is visible, clean and decontaminate receptacles immediately, or as soon as is feasible.
- Always use mechanical means such as tongs, forceps, or a brush and dust plan to pick up contaminated broken glassware; never pick up with hands even if gloves are worn.
- Store or process reusable sharps in a way that ensures safe handling.
- Place other regulated waste, which includes those listed below, in closable and labeled or color-coded containers. When storing, handling, transporting or shipping, place other regulated waste in containers that are constructed to prevent leakage.

  a. Liquid or semi-liquid blood or other potentially infectious materials

  b. Items contaminated with blood or other potentially infectious materials that could release these substances in a liquid or semi-liquid state if compressed

  c. Items caked with dried blood or other potentially infectious materials that are capable of releasing these materials during handling

  d. Contaminated sharps

  e. Pathological and microbiological wastes containing blood or other potentially infectious materials

- When discarding contaminated sharps, place them in containers that are closable, puncture resistant, appropriately labeled or color-coded, and leak proof on the sides and bottoms.
- Ensure that sharps containers are easily accessible to personnel and located as close as is feasible to the immediate area where sharps are used or can be reasonably anticipated to be found. Sharps containers also must be kept upright throughout use, replaced routinely, closed when moved, and not allowed to be overfilled.
- Never manually open, empty, or clean reusable contaminated sharps-disposal containers.
- Discard all regulated waste, as described previously, according to federal, state, and local regulations.
- Handle contaminated laundry as little as possible and with a minimum of agitation.
- Use appropriate personal protective equipment when handling contaminated laundry.
- Place wet contaminated laundry in leakproof, labeled or color-coded containers before transporting.
- Bag contaminated laundry at its location of use.
- Never sort or rinse contaminated laundry in areas of its use.

Labeling

The standard requires waste bags, storage containers, or shipping cartons containing blood, other potentially infectious materials, or regulated waste to be marked with fluorescent orange or orange-red warning labels. The labels are not required when red bags or red containers are used or when several individual containers are placed into a single labeled container during transport. The warning label must contain the biohazard symbol and the word BIOHAZARD (Figures 4.3 and 4.4).

If an Exposure Incident Occurs

An exposure incident is described as a specific eye, mouth, other mucous membrane, non-intact skin, or parenteral contact with blood or other potentially infectious materials that results from the performance of an employee's duties.

As part of their written exposure-control plan, agencies are required to develop procedures for exposure incidents.

When an exposure incident occurs, responders should immediately

- Seek immediate medical attention for a post exposure evaluation

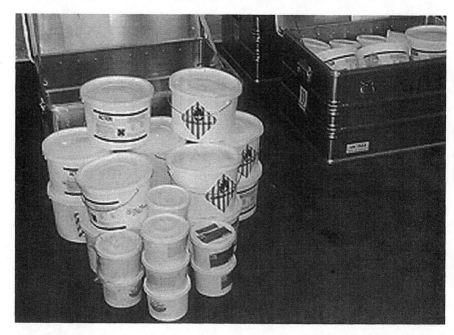

Figure 4.3 Properly labeled hazardous materials, ready for transport as part of a mobile mass fatality incident morgue. (Courtesy of Kenyon International Emergency Services, Inc.)

- Report the exposure incident to a leader

As part of the post-exposure evaluation the following actions should occur.

1. If legally allowed, the source of contamination should be tested for various bloodborne pathogens.*
2. The exposed responder should be provided with test results from the donor source, and advised of the confidentially laws, if applicable.
3. Obtain consent, collect, and test exposed responder's blood as soon as possible after the exposure incident.
4. Determine, based on test, if further treatment or follow-up is warranted.

Following the post-exposure evaluation, the health care professional should provide a written opinion to the exposed responder. Within 15 days

* This is currently a very hot area of debate. As part of pre-incident plans, advice of legal counsel should be sought to provide a legal means to ensure that the donor source can be tested in a timely fashion. Although one might think that since the donor source is no longer living it would not be a contested issue, but that is, unfortunately, not the case.

Figure 4.4 Properly labeled and marked biohazard waste containers ready for transport as part of a mobile mass fatality incident morgue. In the United States, these containers would be red, however, the biohazard symbol is the same worldwide. (Courtesy of Kenyon International Emergency Services, Inc.)

of the post-exposure evaluation the agency must provide a written copy of the report to the exposed responder.

Recordkeeping

There are two types of recordkeeping required by the bloodborne pathogens standard.

1. Medical Records

A confidential medical record for all responders with occupational exposure must be preserved and maintained by their agencies. The records must be maintained in accordance with OSHA's rule governing access to employee-exposure medical records as specified in Title 29, Part 1910.20(e). Medical records must include:

- Responder's name and social security number
- Responder's hepatitis B vaccination status including dates of all hepatitis vaccinations and any medical records related to the individual's ability to receive vaccinations
- Results of examinations, medical testing, and post-exposure evaluation and follow-up procedures

• A copy of health care professionals' written opinions and any information provided to health-care professionals

Medical records must be kept confidential and maintained for at least
the duration of employment plus 30 years.

2. Training Records

Agencies are also required to maintain and keep accurate training records
for three years to include the following:

• Training dates
• Summary of training
• Names and qualifications of trainer(s)
• Names and job titles of trainees

Upon request, both medical and training records must be made available
to various compliance inspectors and the individuals concerned. Additionally, a representative of a responder, with the responder's written consent,
can obtain medical records.

Clearly you can see there are many requirements for those responders
who may be exposed to bloodborne pathogens. However, it at times is a
forgotten or postponed area. I strongly caution both leaders and individuals
to make understanding and compiling with the standard a personal goal.

Federal Requirement—Hazardous Materials

The management of response to incidents involving the release of hazardous
materials, such as large quantities of transportation fuels that may be found
at a incident site or chemical agents released as a result of a train accident, is
generally under the control of the local fire department or hazardous material
unit. Responders focusing on the fatality aspect of the incident should (and
may be required) to have some awareness training on potential hazards.

Clearly, when an incident site has not been rendered safe, search for and
recovery of the bodies should not even begin. It is not wise to risk the living
to recover the dead. If risks must be taken, they should calculated and risk
assessment conducted to make an informed decision.

Please note that the laws involved in this area change rapidly; users should
consult their agency's technical and legal experts.

Nonetheless, the basic requirements for mass fatality incident responders
focusing on tasks related to the deceased, depending on their arrival and
integration into the scene, may include training requirements and "right to
know" requirements.

Written Hazardous Communication Plan

Responders should also be aware that under Title 29, Code of Federal Regulations, Part 1910.1200, it is mandated that employers (agencies) must prepare and maintain a written communication plan.

In part, 1910.1200 states that:

> Employers shall develop, implement, and maintain at each workplace, a written hazard communication program which at least describes how the criteria specified in paragraphs (f), (g), and (h) of this section for labels and other forms of warning, material safety data sheets, and employee information and training will be met, and which also includes the following:
>
> A list of the hazardous chemicals known to be present using an identity that is referenced on the appropriate material safety data sheet (the list may be compiled for the workplace as a whole or for individual work areas); and,
>
> The methods the employer will use to inform employees of the hazards of non-routine tasks (for example, the cleaning of reactor vessels), and the hazards associated with chemicals contained in unlabeled pipes in their work areas.

Additionally, 1910.1200 requires employers who have employees from different areas working in an area they control to include in their plan methods for ensuring that communication of hazards is made available to all employees.

This requirement is also sometime referred to as "the right to know." Basically stated, you should have a written plan that covers such basics as:

- What the risks are

- How to read and understand the Material Safety Data Sheets (MSDS)

- How to handle, use, store, and properly dispose of each chemical

- What training is required and how it is conducted

- Who participated in training, and who conducted the training

In response to a mass fatality incident, two areas may be affected by this requirement. The first is in the mass fatality incident morgue, where several hazardous chemicals are routinely used, and at the incident site itself, which may be contaminated.

Recommended Compliance Strategies

Mass Fatality Incident Morgue

The following should be maintained as part of your mass fatality incident morgue kit.

    a. A binder containing MSDS for all chemicals used or stored in the kit.
    b. A predeveloped brief training package to integrate responders who may not be a regular part of your organization into a mass fatality incident morgue.

Mass Fatality Incident Site

It is impossible to know what chemicals may be present at a mass fatality incident site. Therefore, some actions here are reactive as opposed to proactive; the key however, is to have a plan to address this reality. I recommend the following actions.

- Before any search and recovery activities begin, contact the fire department or hazardous-materials team leader and ascertain what chemicals are present, if any.
- Obtain copies of the MSDS for those chemicals
- Provide the MSDS to responders who will be working at the site
- Comply with any of the requirements established by the MSDS
- Ask the fire department or hazardous-materials team to conduct any needed quick training or review.

Training Requirements

In addition to the requirements of the written hazard communication plan requirements for specific training, certain general training may be required under various sections of Title 29, Code of Federal Regulations, Part 1910 (various subparts).

Various parts of this section require that first responders, generally defined as police, guard service personnel, night watchmen, emergency medical responders including ambulance personnel and others who are likely to discover or respond to emergency incidents involving hazardous substances, receive initial and annual refresher awareness level training. Clearly, most personnel involved in the response will fall into this category.

The training required is targeted at teaching employees to recognize the human hazards present during these emergencies and how to protect themselves against such hazards. The required training also includes how to accurately and fully report the necessary information to an "alarm dispatcher" so that subsequent emergency responders are fully informed. Many first-responder awareness-training courses presently run from 4 to 12 hours, but the standard does not set a mandatory minimum.

As you can see, there are many requirements to ensure the safety and protection of responders. Unfortunately, some people still believe those rules can go out the window during a mass fatality incident response. This just is not true. Some operations have come to a complete standstill while determinations about safety requirements were made and new procedures instituted. The best strategy to avoid these problems is to anticipate them and plan according.

Mass Fatality Incident Exposure Control

There are three stages of exposure control. They are actions taken before an incident occurs, actions accomplished during an incident, and finally actions carried out after an incident. Throughout all the phases, two things are essential. One is that all responders, regardless of rank or position, follow the established safety procedures. The other essential item is that you must have supervisor support. Supervisors must be willing and able to enforce the standards.

Before

This phase of the program, which is an agency responsibility, involves several key areas.

1.Written Exposure Control Plan

As you may recall, the written exposure-control plan establishes certain practices you must follow in the course of your work. These actions address preventive measures such as providing vaccinations. Additionally, as part of your overall programs, you must address who is at risk and what that risk is. Then you must provide training to those at risk.

2.Classes

Schedule regular classes for responders on effective control measures. Again it is a requirement under the law; unfortunately it is often forgotten and allowed to slip lower and lower on the priority scale. Training classes should focus on the *realistic* threat and the value of following standards. A major problem in mass fatality incident response is the *perceived* threat of biological and chemical contamination. Quite often, this perceived threat is based on a lack of knowledge. Even when that threat is minor, as is commonly the case, the lack of understanding and the perception of grave danger will force some agencies to take expensive, time consuming, and risky actions when they are neither appropriate nor required.

3. Train with PPE

Incorporate the use of various levels and types of personal protective equipment into your training programs and exercise drills. Tasks that are very easy while wearing no PPE can be difficult and take longer to accomplish while wearing it. An added benefit is that users should achieve some sense of confidence in the protection afforded by the PPE. This training also allows them to become accustomed to working in the PPE and learning what their limitations are while using it.

4. Vaccinations

Another requirement of the law, but sometimes forgotten. The value of being vaccinated is ultimately realized when the other protective systems fail and an exposure occurs.

During

In this phase, certain actions should occur that require leader involvement to ensure compliance. However, mandatory participation at all levels is a legal requirement. In this phase, all actions are conducted on or near the incident site.

In this phase, incident managers should consider responders who may be coming from different jurisdictions or just simply may be volunteers who have offered to help. As part of pre-incident plans, agency leaders should get together and establish minimum standards for all personnel who may become involved in an incident response.

1. Written Exposure-Control Plan

The written exposure-control plan establishes certain practices you must follow in the course of your work. These actions address universal precautions, housekeeping, work, and place controls. Following those procedures is the best path you can take.

2. Controlled Site

Once the focus of the incident switches from life and property preservation to recovery of the deceased, complete site control should be established. Incident managers should invoke all available health-code regulations, which often allow a mass fatality incident site to be declared a biological hazard area, thereby effectively limiting media access.

Any personnel entering the site should be checked to ensure they have proper PPE and that they have valid identification.

As part of site control, individuals who have not had vaccinations, training, or experience with exposure to contamination but have a valid need to enter the site should be given a quick familiarization program and training on the PPE, and afforded the opportunity to receive vaccinations. Naturally, these actions should be documented. Ideally, these individuals will not have a great role in the response and therefore the actions are merely precautionary.

3. Decontamination Stations

When warranted, establish, in conjunction with controlled entry points, areas specifically for the decontamination of responders leaving the incident site. The stations may not have to be anything sophisticated, they may be as simple as a wash area and an area to remove grossly contaminated gloves and coveralls. Or they can include showers and clothing-exchange points. It will depend on the various types and levels of contamination.

4. Proper Use of PPE

Ensure that responders have and properly use the available PPE, and that any person working with remains is following universal precautions. Look at the PPE supplies; ensure that the right sizes and types are readily available. Make on-the-spot corrections or remove those individuals who choose not to follow the guidelines.

5. Defined Work Areas

As discussed in the requirements of the exposure control plan, ensure that areas in which contamination is present or is likely to be present, have proper controls in place. In other words, break areas should be away from work areas, preferably with a wash station in between.

Although most, if not all, these suggestions sound simple and are based on common sense, you must remember that at any mass fatality site you will have, in areas likely to contain contamination, a multitude of people. Although most of these people may meet the basic qualifications for entry into the site, in reality they may know very little about the law and the benefits of following health and safety standards.

Therefore, it is imperative that you have established simple procedures to minimize the risk of exposure.

After

The concern for exposure to contamination does not end with the incident. Fortunately, following some basic, preestablished procedures can make this an easy phase.

1. **Written Exposure Control Plan**

   As you may recall, the written exposure-control plan establishes certain after-action follow-up procedures. These should address how to follow up on individuals who had exposure incident, as well as basic cleaning and sanitation requirements and disposal of contaminated material. Following those procedures is the best after-action you can do. Some specific procedures are as follows.

2. **Site Clearance**

   Before any site is released to contractors to begin cleanup or restoration, incident managers should ensure that all remains have been recovered. Several repetitive sweeps of an area may be required. This is especially true in large open areas with where a high-speed impact has scattered wreckage and body parts over a large area.

   If an area is contaminated with other than biological contamination, specialized firms should be brought in to effect a clean-up operation. Commonly, most mass fatality incident sites are now converted into formal or even informal memorial areas.

3. **Equipment and Facilities Decontamination or Disposal**

   The recent trend has been to dispose of many of the materials used in incident response, from the portable tents used to house mass fatality incident morgues to equipment used during recovery operations. In some cases, this may be more economical than decontaminating the items. However, there is often a cost for disposal of contaminated items. These factors will have to be considered when making your decision.

   When establishing your operations, consideration should be given to the actions required to later decontaminate the facilities and equipment. Care should be taken to acquire items and facilities that are easy to decontaminate.

4. **Exposure Control and Personal Effects**

   An often-forgotten aspect of mass fatality incidents is the disposition of personal effects. In many cases, such items may have been contaminated with biological or chemical contaminates. Because of this, some very important decisions will have to be made. It is easy to make these decisions as pre-incident plans. Items to consider are as follows.

- *What does the law require?*

In some cases, various laws may require that all personal effects be recovered. If the person(s) authorized to receive those effects wants them back, then they must be decontaminated.

- *What items will be decontaminated?*

Will attempts be made to decontaminate all items or only those items, such as nonporous materials, that are easily decontaminated? If that is the case, will items such as letters or papers be photocopied so the copies can be returned in lieu of the originals?

- *Who will pay for the decontamination?*

Again, in some cases the law is very specific. But in other cases, usually when no single responsible party can be identified and held financially accountable, such as following a terrorist attack, will the local jurisdiction absorb the cost?

- *What actions will be taken to prevent further contamination of personal effects?*

Such actions as immediately placing into plastic bags uncontaminated effects recovered on a body (ensuring that those effects stay with the body all the way to the mass fatality incident morgue) or immediate collection of effects from the incident site can have a draw on limited resources. However, they may make it easier to effect disposition of those items at a later date.

If the decision is made to hold all items, regardless of contamination, and process them for disposition after an incident, then incident managers or third-party contractors must be aware that they will have to follow the procedures established for occupational exposure to bloodborne pathogens and perhaps for occupational exposure to hazardous materials.

In no event should contaminated items be returned to any person authorized to receive the personal effects. This not only because of the health risks, but more so the emotional damage done when someone receives an item that has dried blood or other bloody fluids or tissue on it. Incredibly, this has occurred in previous incidents.

Mass Fatality Responder Liability

Currently, the courts have dismissed most cases against individuals and agencies acting under the flag of office. In other cases, jurisdictions have settled cases, without admitting liability, to avoid costly and lengthy legal battles. However, with the increase in legal firms that specialize in mass fatality incidents, it is apparent that the trend may move from suing the party or parties responsible for causing, or contributing, to the incident, to the agency and individual responders involved in the response.

Here the value of pre-incident planning and training is demonstrated again. Times are changing; standards of response are changing. With every incident, the general public has a better understanding and, as a result of that understanding, certain expectations of what should occur during an incident response. When those expectations are not met, legislation is developed to mandate the meeting of expectations, and when that fails, lawsuits occur.

An additional area for incident managers to consider is whether they assume liability for actions committed by individuals from other supporting agencies acting on behalf of a requesting agency in response to a mass fatality incident. In some cases, individuals are protected, such as under the Federal Response Plan, and responders are not liable for any claim for performance. However, does that liability transfer over to the lead agency? Such questions should be referred to appropriate legal counsel and answers established long before an incident so that appropriate pre-incident agreements can be drafted and agreed upon.

Summary

Most countries have fairly specific laws and regulations regarding exposure to bloodborne pathogens and hazardous materials. These laws and regulations apply even in the response to a mass fatality incident. Frankly, given the increased risk and scope of the response, it would be risky to not follow established protocols. A successful plan involves ensuring that good policies are in place and that such policies are followed by all involved in the incident. A special challenge is to incorporate those individuals from outside your agency who may have different standards and ensure they are provided with the required equipment and trained in its use and other required actions.

Incident mangers should also give thought to defining liability for performance during response and ensure that they have taken all necessary steps to mitigate that liability for themselves, their responders, and their agencies.

Search and Recovery Operations

5

In this chapter, we begin to focus on the actual response operations. Response operations focus on those areas that represent the actual activities taken once life and property preservation comes to an end and the focus moves to the search, recovery, morgue operations and final disposition of the deceased and their personal effects.

Search Overview

Search operations for this guide refer to locating, marking the location, establishing a grid system, if necessary, and assigning a search number to each body or body part located. In this chapter, personal effects refer to those items found on or immediately adjacent to these remains.

Before beginning your search operation, a key point to remember is that the goal is to be able to establish a confirmed identification of each person, associate any body parts with a particular individual, document any injury pattern, and complete required investigations. The search and subsequent documentation of the search may play a key role in accomplishing those goals. The guiding force is the ability to recreate the scene, and preservation of evidence (Figure 5.1).

Executing a speedy search and quickly moving the remains to a mass fatality morgue, while certainly ensuring that the dead are no longer exposed to the public view and the elements, may actually result in a longer identification time, loss of valuable information, and a lack of complete reports.

Figure 5.1 Devastation typical of a high-speed rail accident. Note the damage to both rail cars and surrounding houses. (Courtesy of Kenyon International Emergency Services, Inc.)

Possible Benefits of a Controlled Search Action

Identification

When fragmented remains are recovered, it is important to be able to ascertain which other fragments were recovered nearby. That information can provide the ME with a starting point to begin association of fragmented remains. Additionally, personal effects located on or immediately adjacent to remains may help to establish a tentative identification.

While neither of these actions will provide a confirmed identification, they may offer a place to begin.

Criminal Proceedings

Months or even years later, during criminal proceedings, questions often arise about exact locations of specific individuals who may have been more than just victims. The ability to establish the facts of the individual's involvement may rest on being able to pinpoint their recovery location.

Incident Investigations

As part of a comprehensive accident investigation, it is often important to know the location of various crew members, whether it is a flight crew, train engineers, or boat crew. Were they recovered where they were expected to be or was it somewhere entirely different?

It is important to know what occurred prior to the incident. In other words, after completion of the medicolegal autopsy and the plotting of individual toxicology reports on a map does a pattern appear that perhaps suggest fumes of noxious gases were present in a certain area of a vessel?

Remains that were located in a certain grouping may at the medicolegal autopsy indicate a peculiar or unique injury pattern. This information, used in conjunction with other details, may help to establish, confirm, or exclude a probable explanation for the incident.

Recovery Overview

This simply refers to the process of moving the bodies, fragments, or personal effects from the incident site to the mass fatality incident morgue. Some incident managers and agencies may want to have these functions accomplished as two separate operations. .

Figure 5.2 Large debris field from a ground impact aircraft accident. (Courtesy of Kenyon International Emergency Services, Inc.)

Figure 5.3 Commercial transportation helicopter being lifted onto a salvage vessel. Several remains and personal effects were recovered inside the wreckage. (Courtesy of Kenyon International Emergency Services, Inc.)

Search Basics

Clearly, the type of incident and the incident location, along with the number of deceased will have an impact on how you manage your search and recovery. No two mass fatality incidents are the same nor are the responses; there are, however, some commonalties among the responses.

Aircraft Accident, Ground Recovery

Aircraft accidents resulting in ground impacts or debris landing on the ground often result from mid-air collisions, accidents that occur on take off and landing, or explosions. Usually these result in high-energy impacts that may include pre-crash fires as well as fire resulting from the impact. Debris fields are often large and remains and effects are found buried in the ground, hidden beneath wreckage, in demolished ground structures, in trees and bushes, and are often fragmented (Figure 5.2).

Aircraft Accident, Water Recovery

Aircraft accidents resulting in water impacts or debris landing on the water often result from mid-air collisions, accidents on take off and landing, or explosions set to occur once the craft is over the water (Figure 5.3) Usually these result in high-energy impacts that may include pre-crash fires. Debris fields are often large and obviously do not remain static. Recoveries may occur on the surface of the water, on shore if the craft impacts close enough for the remains to be washed to shore, or by divers conducting recovery operations underwater on the wreckage. Depending on the water temperature, decomposition can be hastened, and additional trauma caused by various sea animals.

Building Collapse

Building collapse can be the result of intentional acts such as bombings; or because of accidents, sometimes related to faulty construction; or as result of a natural disaster such as an earthquake or landslide (Figure 5.4). Remains are often extremely difficult to recover and usually those conducting the search and recovery are at risk of injury from falling or collapsing debris. Recovery can take days and even weeks. Remains recovery may actually begin while crews continue to search and, in some cases, recover survivors.

Figure 5.4 Partial building collapse following a terrorist attack on a major metropolitan area. The building was searched by an urban search and rescue (USAR) team. (author's collection)

Additional concerns are caused when remains may be partially visible in the wreckage, but may actually still take days to recover because they are partially buried underneath rubble. At some point, a decision may have to be made to bring down any standing part of the building prior to continuing search and recovery efforts.

Ship Accidents

Although not as common as mass fatality incidents aboard aircraft, mass fatality incidents do occur on passenger ships. These incidents are often a result of fire on board the ship, collision with another ship or object, or the ship flounders for a variety of reasons. If the ship does not sink, recoveries are better accomplished once the vessel has been towed to a sheltered area or port and stabilized. In these cases, remains will mostly likely be found in common areas. Not all remains may be recovered. In cases where the ship sinks, some remains and personal effects may be recovered floating on the surface, and still others found in the wreckage (Figure 5.5).

Figure 5.5 Wreckage of a partially submerged auto and passenger ferry. This vessel should be righted and secured before search and recovery efforts can begin. (Courtesy of Kenyon International Emergency Services, Inc.)

Train Accidents

Mass fatality incidents occurring on trains are most often a result of a high-speed impact involving two trains or a train derailment. In both cases, remains are often extremely difficult to recover and usually those conducting the search and recovery are at risk for injury from falling or collapsing debris. Recovery can take days and even weeks. Remains recovery may actually begin while search crews continue and some cases recover survivors (Figure 5.6).

This list is by no means complete. Smaller-scale mass fatality incidents occur in mass murders or smaller accidents, and, although when taken in its

Figure 5.6 High-speed rail accident. Condition of the wreckage will make search and recovery difficult and hazardous for responders. (Courtesy of Kenyon International Emergency Services, Inc.)

entirety, the response effort could overwhelm a local jurisdiction, the actual search and recovery will most likely not be that difficult.

Number of Deceased

When determining the type of search to be used, incident managers must look at the number of expected fatalities. In incidents spread out over large areas with few fatalities, searchers can be spread out farther apart. Incidents involving a large number of deceased will require a larger number of people to be involved in the search.

Search Patterns

After looking at the incident site and terrain, the incident manager must determine which search pattern or combination of patterns to use. Various patterns exist, but the type of incident and terrain might very well limit the patterns you use. The type of search pattern used does not matter as much as does the fact that the search must be systematic and thorough. Ideally, multiple teams will search each area to ensure no remains or fragments are left behind. The search should be conducted during daylight. Even then, additional lighting may be needed. In building searches, when looking for the living, search actively should, and often does, continue through the night until no hope of rescuing survivors exists.

We will only address building, train, ship, and open-terrain searches, as they are typically accomplished using regular responders who complete a variety of tasks. Searches conducted in the water are very specialized and almost always conducted with the assistance of highly trained naval or Coast Guard units.

Building Searches

A plan of the building or buildings to be searched should be acquired or, if none is available, made from interviews of people who are familiar with the site.

Survivors of the collapse and people who have knowledge of the inside layout should be interviewed to determine the following:
- The usual pre-incident location of each known victim
- The last known pre-incident location of each victim

That information should then be plotted onto the floor plan.

Additional information, such as the type of office or function of a par-ticular office should be plotted on the floor plan. An engineer should super-impose the remaining structure onto the floor plan to provide an image of the building as it currently exists, and then number the remaining major support beams or walls and place that number on the floor plan as well as the original support beams or walls.

The search should then begin. The flow of the search will be determined by what areas are safe to work in. The start and end points are totally dependent on the building and the extent of its damage. Search and recovery can originate from the roof and upper floors of the building and through a basement or parking garage at the same time.

These points will be brought up again when we discuss gridding the site.

Train Wreckage

The type of search used here again is limited by the condition of the wreckage. A simple search pattern that has search teams starting at opposite ends of a rail car or specific area, if rail cars are recognizable, and finishing at the other end of each rail car or specific area is often sufficient.

Ships

Ship searches are similar to building searches in that they usually have fixed entry and exit points. In searching ships, building plans or a ship's layout should be acquired. Likely location for the remains should be plotted as well as hazardous areas. Multiple search teams should enter the ship and search only one level or deck at a time. Search teams should converge on a central location and then continue through areas searched by the previous team.

Open Terrain

To begin, the parameters of the area to be searched should be established. Using a map of the area, the incident managers should place a boundary around the entire debris field. There should be a several-hundred-yard overlap from where the debris field ends and the boundary markers are established. Large areas should then be broken into quadrants for the purpose of conducting a search.

The easiest search type for open terrain is the open formation in which searchers form a side-by-side line, usually with several feet of open space between them. They then move forward at an equal pace; the search team leader moves behind the line to control it and ensure that no one gets ahead of or behind another.

In areas with a limited line of sight, a closed formation is used. It is similar to the open formation, except searchers are no farther than arm's distance from each other.

In this formation, searchers line up and move forward through the site. Once they reach the opposite boundary, if another team is unavailable, the searchers should then switch places with each other and search the area again.

There are other search patterns that can be used, but for open terrain I strongly recommend the above.

Search Sequence

Before any section is searched, the following preliminary actions should occur.

1. Document the Entire Scene

The entire scene should be photographed using both still and video, color, and black and white. Using black and white is necessary because if the incident results in litigation, color photographs are sometimes not allowed because they are considered too shocking for the jury.

2. Establish Perimeters

Initial boundaries and perimeters should be established. As mentioned earlier, boundaries should be established several hundred yards after the end of the debris field. Large areas should be sectioned into quadrants. The overall boundaries and quadrants should be clearly marked.

3. Assessment of Hazards

After getting a look at the overall scene and talking with other incident managers and specialists such as fire and HAZMAT personnel, the search leader should assess what the hazards are and what actions should be taken to mitigate them. Areas to look at include the presence of bloodborne pathogens, chemical contamination of the site, wreckage, and possibly harmful animals such as snakes or other types that might inhabit the incident site.

After those actions are complete, each search team leader should complete the following:

4. Assemble and Brief Search Team

a. Each search team should be composed of

- **Team Leader.** Team leaders are responsible for the search teams. They assign positions, ensure all needed equipment is available and properly used, and that all procedures are followed.
- **Team Scribe.** The scribes are responsible for issuing case numbers.
- **Searchers.** The searchers are responsible for:
  Locating the remains or fragments
  Marking the site with a flag or paint with the assigned case number
  Placing a tag with the case number on the remains or fragments
  Placing the remains or fragments into a human-remains pouch
  Marking the human-remains pouch with the assigned case number
- **Search Team Photographers.** The search-team photographers should photograph each body or fragment before and after a case-number tag has been affixed or placed next to it. These photos are different from the initial photographs of the site, which are more of an overview and not specifically of each body or fragment.
- **Recovery Personnel.** These people assist in placing the bodies, fragments, and personal effects into the human-remains pouches or plastic bags. They also carry the litters to the recovery staging area.

b. Personnel assigned to the team should gather. The team leaders should brief all team members on the following:
- What to expect at the site
- Each team member's specific job
- The site hazards
- The numbering procedure to be used
- The color-coding to be used
- At this time, incident managers from other agencies should brief the search team as to items of interest to their particular organization. Although the primary function of this team is finding the fatalities, searchers will often come upon useful investigatory objects, such as a maintenance records, flight books, or obvious explosive-device components. The other agencies' incident managers should provide instruction for either marking the item or notifying the appropriate agency of the find.
- A quick training session can also be conducted on the search pattern and a dry run on how to issue a case number, mark the recovery location, and place the bodies or fragments into the human-remains pouch.

5. Draw equipment
Equipment should be collected from the logistics section or brought to the scene by the individual responders.

A detailed listing is provided in Appendix A.

For the majority of recoveries, the basic equipment listed below is usually sufficient to accomplish the basic search and recovery functions. For very difficult recoveries, such as those from wreckage or very dangerous terrain, technical responders trained to use heavy and specialized tools should be brought in to complete the recovery.

Litters

Bodies or fragments should never be carried using only the straps on the human-remains pouches as this may cause additional damage to the remains, especially those that lack skeletal integrity to support the weight of the body.

Human-Remains Pouches

Pouches should be durable and opaque. Different sizes should be available for children, adults, and fragments. The human-remains pouches should have full center zippers and double reinforced handles.

Various Pin Flags/Various Colors of Spray Paint

As part of your pre-incident plans, or decided on site, colors should be assigned to denote certain things such as remains, personal effects, key wreckage, and recovery boundaries.

These colors should be coordinated with other agencies to ensure that the same colors are not used to denote different things. The purpose of this is to enable search teams to place color-coded flags at recovery sites. Later, when the site is videotaped and possibly gridded, one can immediately tell by looking at the flags the dispersal pattern or recovery location. The paint is used in locations where pin flags cannot be placed.

Tags

I recommend you use Tyvek® tags. They are made of a very durable, paper-like substance that does not readily disintegrate when exposed to liquids. The tags used should be large enough to be easily read and should have twine already attached to the tag.

Writing/Note Supplies

Clipboards, paper, pens for the scribe and searchers. These items are used to record case number, writing the case number on the tags or flags, and for making any notes

Radios

The team leader and scribes should have radios. The team leader should have communication with the incident manager and other team leaders. The scribes should have communication with each other and other search-team scribes to ensure that duplicate numbers are not issued.

Cameras

The preferred camera is a high-quality, 35mm single-lens reflex (SLR), 28–80 mm lens, and a mounted flash. Various speeds of film should be available to account for varying light conditions. Remember, these pictures may be used in criminal proceedings, in hearings to refute or support incident causation theories, or as a record on incident response.

Plastic Bags (Various Sizes)

Any of the commercial food-storage bags will work just fine. These bags will be used to protect personal effects from further environmental or body fluid damage, maintain group integrity of items recovered near or on a body, and to hold small amounts of substances that could possibly be human tissue.

Personal Protective Equipment and Personal Care Items

Any required items to meet the OSHA standard and items for personal comfort such as hats, rain gear, insect repellent, and drinking water. Naturally, contaminated gloves should be removed and hands and face area sanitized before the consumption of any water. As keeping hydrated is very important and requires frequent drinks it is not practical to have searchers leave the site. Therefore they must take basic precautions before drinking the water. However, the same does not good for food or tobacco products. Searchers should not consume those on site and should stop for food and if necessary tobacco breaks (*Author's note: tobacco use is a contraindication to staying healthy and thereby reducing the effects of incident stress, many responders use tobacco and it is unrealistic to not address the use.*)

6. Enter the Site

The team, which has now been assembled, briefed, issued the required equipment, and dressed in appropriate personal protective equipment should now enter the site.

Both team scribe and site security should note exact time they enter the site.

7. Search and Recover Sequence

   a. Searchers get into whatever search formation or pattern is appropriate.
   b. Searchers move out.
   c. Remains OR personal effects are located. (Note: Commingled remains should never be separated at the incident site. Separation should occur only in the mass fatality incident morgue. If the commingled remains do not fit into a human-remains pouch, a plastic sheet wrapped in a cloth sheet should be used to provide covering and protection. In the same way, fragments, no matter how similar they appear, should never be associated with any other remains at the incident site (Figure 5.7).
   d. Write the case number on one tag.
   e. Write the case number on one pin flag or site marker.

Notes on case numbers: You should use whatever system you are comfortable with, but remember the best system is often the simplest. Whatever system you use, it should:

   • Account for remains recovered at the site
   • Account for remains received from local medical treatment facilities
   • Account for remains recovered weeks after the incident
   • Provide a quick count of the total number recovered at any one point

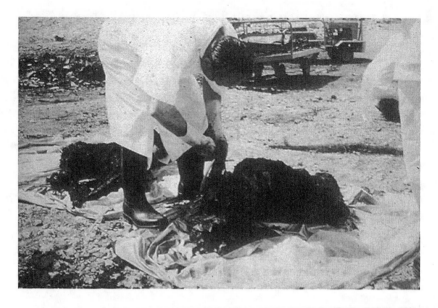

(a)

(b)

Figure 5.7 Examples of commingled remains. (a) Remains are being recovered from an incident site; (b) a forensic specialist examines the remains in a controlled fashion. Both photos show the devastation and challenges typical of a fire scene. Remains will be moved as recovered and examined in a controlled area. (Courtesy of Kenyon International Emergency Services, Inc.)

- Be easily identifiable as belonging to a mass fatality incident victim, as opposed to a "regular" fatality

The system I recommend has been used quite often with great success. Most medical examiner's systems use a sequential number assigned to each body or fragment as it is entered into the ME system. The number usually consists of the year followed by a dash and then the sequential number. For example 98-151 would denote the 151st body or fragment received into the ME system in 1998.

To use that system for a mass fatality incident I recommend that you look at the previous year's final number, add a "buffer" or separating number, which would be dependent upon how far into the year you are, and start the mass fatality number system there.

For example, Anytown had 373 remains entered into its ME system last year (1998) The last case number issued was 98-373. Anytown uses a calendar year for recordkeeping. During April 1999, Anytown has a mass fatality incident; the medical examiner should look at the previous year's total, in this case 98-373. He should then add a buffer number. I would base the buffer on the number of living victims rescued from the mass fatality incident and evacuated to a medical treatment facility. Some of those people may yet die and they would be assigned case numbers in sequence with the mass fatality incident. In the example, no one survived the incident so I would use the number 20 just to account for any unexpected yearly increases.

Anytown's first mass fatality incident case number will be 99-393. Using this system, Anytown's ME can quickly separate the mass fatality incident case number from the "regular" fatalities.

Other systems I have seen involved assigning the number 1 to the first remains found and just going sequentially as each additional person or item is recovered or received into the system.

    f. Attach tag to the body, fragment, or effect.
    g. Place pin flag or marker in the ground or spray paint the number on the ground or object.
    h. Record the information on the log.
    i. Place the item into the human-remains pouch or plastic bag.
    j. Paint or write the case number on the human-remains pouch or plastic bag.
    k. Place the human-remains pouch or plastic bag on a litter.
    l. Move the litter to the recovery staging area for movement to the mass fatality incident morgue.
    m. Re-photograph the area.
    n. Continue with the search.

8. Recovery Staging Area.

Here, the remains and effects are staged for movement to the mass fatality incident morgue. Movement can be accomplished in individual removal vehicles or a number of items can be placed into a refrigeration trailer and moved as a group to the mass fatality incident morgue.

An advantage to using the refrigerated trailer for movement is that refrigeration will slow decomposition, and you will not require as many movement resources. Additionally, if the mass fatality incident morgue is not yet prepared, they should not be moved to that location.

The biggest disadvantage is that you can easy overload the morgue by moving a large number of items to the receiving section at one time. Ideally, they should be staggered.

Regardless of the method you use, attention must be paid to certain details. They are:

- The case number on the human-remains pouch should be checked against the case number on the tag attached to the remains or fragment.
- A log should be maintained noting when the items left the incident site, in which vehicle they left, and the name of the vehicle operator.
- Removal vehicles or refrigerated vans should not have visible names or identifying features; they always move under law enforcement escort.

All in all, these are pretty basic details. Depending on the site terrain and the number and condition of the fatalities, the search can move along at a steady pace. The key is to be systematic, thorough, and have built-in system checks to catch mistakes before they impact the response.

Gridding

Once the search and recovery effort is complete. Action should be taken to document and establish in a usable form the exact location of remains or personal effects. The end product should be a computer-generated site map or diagram with recovery locations clearly denoted. Once confirmed identifications have been established, the map should be updated to correlate the names to the numbers. The maps or diagrams are best produced using a simple computer aided design (CAD) program.

Gridding a site is the process of establishing the exact location of any item to include slope and distance from an established point. When all items have been plotted, one can then determine the relationships, if any, between and among them.

A variety of methods can be used to collect the required data. The common methods and equipment used include global positioning systems (GPS), various survey positioning devices (survey theodolite transit or Total Station®), or establishing a union grid (in which an actual grid structure is constructed on site).

To determine the best method or combination of methods to use, the incident manager should study the site terrain and the number and condition of remains. Generally, the following parameters can help you make a decision.

If you are going to use survey equipment and surveyors, it is important to ensure that the incident managers and surveyors speak the same language. Some basic terms to understand are

Coordinate data—Consists of numeric digits that represent a specific geographical location. The coordinates are arrived at after getting the northing and easting/westing or the southing and easting/westing, whichever the case may be.
Northing: the latitudinal difference between two positions as a result of moving north (the datum point and the pin flag.)
Southing: the latitudinal difference between two positions as a result of moving south (the datum point and the pin flag.)
Easting: the longitudinal difference between two positions as result of moving east (the datum point and the pin flag.)
Westing: the longitudinal difference between two positions as result of moving east (the datum point and the pin flag.)
Declination adjustment—The adjustment made to the surveyor instruments to account for the difference between true north and magnetic north.
Raw data—The two angles (direction) and distance from the surveyors' equipment to the pin flag. The raw data has to be converted to coordinate data before it is useful.
Datum point—This is the point from which all measurements originate. Ideally, this should be a known location with a semi-permanent or prominent feature. If you are in an area without a known point, establish one by relaying angles from visible features or contact your local geographical survey for help.

Open Terrain Incidents (Majority of Remains Intact)

In incidents when the majority of the bodies are intact and the ground slopes gently, so as to allow a direct line of sight from a central location to the majority of remains and fragments, a surveyor's theodolite transit or Total Station® is the best device to use (Figure 5.8).

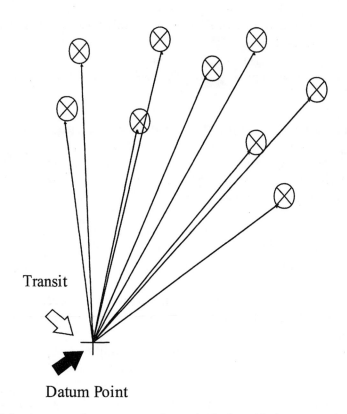

Transit

Datum Point

Figure 5.8 Diagram showing a simple method of establishing exact location of remains, personal effects, or wreckage in an open area. The circled X's represent each discovery, and the straight lines represent the azimuth to each as determined by the survey device. In this case, the datum point is selected, the survey device is placed over it, and the distance and azimuth to the remains or personal effect is determined and recorded.

In this operation, the theodolite or Total Station® is placed in a central location that can be easy located at any time such as over a benchmarker, major road intersection, or prominent point. A person using a handheld measuring rod, or reflective prism mounted on a rod, places the base of the rod at the marker flag. The individual operating the theodolite or Total Station⁽ makes a reading of the information from the theodolite or makes entries into Total Station®

The information collected will depend on the device used. At a minimum, it should include

- The distance from the known object (Theodolite/Total Station®) to the remains

- The horizontal-angle deviation from baseline (the total number of degrees right or left from the baseline or backsite, usually expressed as zero)
- The vertical-angle deviation relative to level, most often expressed as zeros, and level being a 90°angle.

Today, many surveyor's theodolite transits are electronic and provide digital reading of the data, which reduces the error rate in reading the data from the various dials on the older models. Either way, the data must then be noted to the specific case number the readings were taken for and later entered into a CAD program.

A distinct advantage of the Total Station® is that the date is automatically recorded onto a magnetic card, which can be then downloaded to a computer and easily opened and read by various CAD programs. The data is stored as a read-only file so it cannot be changed. When you are working with the data it is always saved into another file. This can be a very important point in criminal proceedings. The disadvantage, of course, is the cost.

Documenting recovery location is actually very easy this way and very accurate.

Limited-Line-of-Site Incidents (Majority of Remains Intact)

In incidents where the majority of remains are intact, but are widely dispersed, or the terrain is very uneven and has a limited line of sight, then a global-positioning system is the best way to go.

Using this method, an operator carrying GPS device will go to each pin flag and record the data from the GPS. A word of caution, GPS devices currently available on the open market and to most law enforcement agencies have a deliberate offset error programmed into them. This has been done to protect military technology and ensure the devices are not used for the wrong purposes. Therefore, if the degree of error is unacceptable, attempt to have local military personnel come to the site and use one of their GPS devices to collect the data.

The information collected will depend on the device used. At a minimum, it should include:

- The exact grid coordinate of the pin flag or site marker
- The elevation of the pin flag or site marker

Buildings/Ships

In incidents when the majority of remains are located inside structures, the recovery location should be expressed relative to a fixed point in the structure.

Once measurements are taken they should again be transferred to a copy of the building plans or scale diagrams.

Open Terrain Incidents (Gross Fragmentation)

In incidents when the majority of remains are fragmented, commingled, and intermingled with the wreckage, an overlaying union grid system may be the only way to accurately and completely document the recovery location. Some drawbacks to this method are that it is time intensive to establish—depending on the terrain and size of the area to be gridded, this operation can take days. It requires some skill, as lines must be placed, markers established and placed, and numerous measurements taken. In the method's favor, it allows for expansion and can radiate in any direction. .

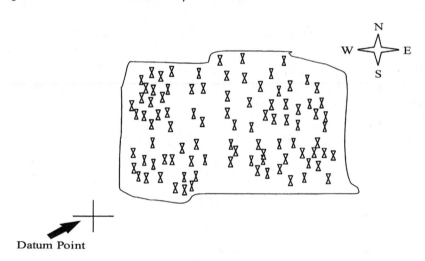

Figure 5.9 Diagram showing establishment of a datum point. (*Note:* X's represent remains, wreckage, or personal effects.)

Once the decision has been made to establish a union grid, the sequence is as follows:

1. Establish a Datum Point

The datum point is the location from which all measurements are taken (Figure 5.9). With luck, it is already a known location. Ideally, it should be in one corner of the site, although that is not compulsory. Such a location will, however, make establishing the grid easier. A union grid is based on the cardinal points, in that the baseline and meridian line are established on the four points of the compass.Note that the cardinal directions are noted in the upper right hand corner with north pointing up. This is the standard way of orienting a union grid.

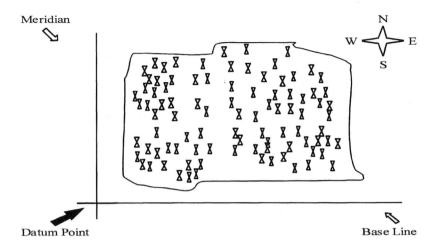

Figure 5.10 Diagram showing establishment of a base line and meridian line.

In the next step, a baseline will be established. The baseline will go 90° east or 90° (compass reading of 270°) west. In some circumstances, the union grid will radiate out around the datum point. However, as mentioned earlier, it is better to start in a corner and move up and out.

2. **Establish a Baseline and Meridian Line**
A baseline is the line running parallel to the earth's latitude lines, or east and west. The meridian line runs parallel to the earth's longitude lines, or north and south (Figure 5.10)
   - A baseline with a heading of 90° has been laid out.
   - Then a meridian line with a heading of 0° or 360°, as you prefer, is laid out.
   - Colored nylon twine should be used as the line.
   - Tall (2-ft) tent stakes should be used as opposed to survey stakes, as the normal tendency is for people to trip and knock down the stakes while moving around the site, therefore strong stakes are essential.
   - Stakes to hold the line should be placed at intervals to provide needed support and tension on the line.
   - A tall (8-ft) stake and flag should be placed at the end of the baseline twine so it is clearly visible to anyone working on the site. This helps to define and establish the boundaries.

In the next phase, grid squares will be established.

Establish Grid Square Markers

Once you have laid out the baseline and gridline, you should then determine the size of your union grid squares. The size is dependent upon the terrain; the number and condition of the bodies, and the density of the bodies in any one area. For this illustration, we will use a grid area of 25 ft by 25 ft. You can use whatever size you prefer. I would not, however, go much larger than 40 ft square, as that defeats the purpose of using a union grid (Figure 5.11).

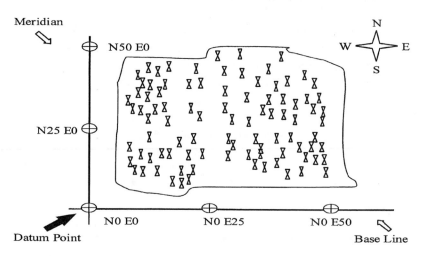

Figure 5.11 Diagram showing establishment of 25-meter grid squares.

- For this illustration we have decided to make the grid 25 ft square.
- A tent stake is placed 25 ft due east (90°) on the base line. The tent stake is inscribed with the letters and numbers N0, for north 0 ft, and E25, for east 25 ft.
- Additional tent stakes are placed at 25-ft intervals, due east (90°) on the base line. Continue out as far as necessary to provide the coverage you desire.
- Each tent stake is then inscribed with N0, for north 0 ft, and then EXX, the XX standing for 50, 75, 100, 125, 150, etc. for east 50 ft, 75 ft, 100 ft, and so on.
- Colored nylon twine is then attached to each stake.
- A tent stake is then placed 25 ft due north (0° or 360°) on the meridian line, the letters and numbers N25, for north 25 ft, and E0 for east 0 ft.
- Additional tent stakes are placed at 25 ft intervals, due north (0° or 360°) on the meridian line. Continue out as far as necessary to provide the coverage you desire.

- Each tent stake is then inscribed with NXX, the XX standing for 50, 75, 100, 125, 150, etc., for north 50 ft, 75 ft, 100 ft, and so on, and E0 for east 0 ft.
- Colored nylon twine is then attached to each stake.
- The colored nylon twine attached to N25 E0 is walked east 25 ft.
- The colored nylon twine attached to N0 E25 is walked north 25 ft.
- When the colored nylon twine intersects, the spot is staked.

You can also use the survey equipment for this. To check the accuracy and ensure your grid square is square, use the Pythagorean Theorem. Applied here, the square of the length of the diagonal (measurement from one corner to opposite corner) will equal the sum of the squares of two perpendicular sides. Another method to determine if your square is "square" is to simply measure both diagonals. When the distances are equal, you have a square.)

- That stake should be inscribed N25, for north 25 ft and E 25, for east 25 ft.
- This grid square can now be designated with either a letter or number or a combination. Remember to keep it simple.
- This process is repeated as necessary.

4. Establish Additional Grid Squares

Now that you have established the first grid squares, the rest will go along very easily. Figure 5.12 will give you an idea of what your site should look like.

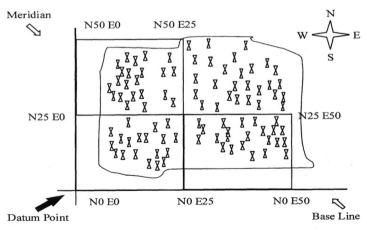

Figure 5.12 Diagram showing complete 25-meter grid squares laid out.

5. Determine Pin Flag Location

Once a grid square has been established, it is then possible to establish an exact location of each pin flag, and consequently the remains or personal effect the flag represents.

There are many ways to accomplish that. The simplest method is to triangulate.

- Measure the distance from two corners to the object.
- The intersection of the two measurements at the pin flag is the location of the item.
- This method without further work does not allow for the measurement of elevation.

Another method to accomplish this is to move the surveyor's theodolite transit or Total Station® over each stake, thereby making each stake a datum point. Measurements can then be taken to each pin flag. This method will allow for determining elevation.

Search Resources

Various groups of responders from different agencies can provide support for search and recovery teams. Because of the survey equipment or GPS devices, gridding teams are somewhat more specialized and should be experienced personnel.

Whether a grid or detailed recovery map or diagram is done or not, certain people should always be part of the response team.

Forensic Anthropologist.   This specialist is invaluable in identifying human from non-human remains.

Forensic Photographer.   Since you are not using instant film, there is no room for error in photographing the remains.

Death Investigator.   Death investigators will be most familiar with recovery of the deceased. They usually understand the OSHA requirements and have been exposed to a variety of remains in varying conditions.

Other team members can be drawn from various agencies such as:

- Sworn Law Enforcement
- Fire Department (especially if doing structure recoveries)
- Funeral Directors
- Military

Volunteer SAR Teams (many jurisdictions include teenagers on their search and rescue teams; I would never allow a young person to work in any area involving remains. Although they might have encountered death before, they should not have to see and deal with a mass fatality incident.)

Cadaver/Body Dog Teams (usually associated with various national search and recovery organizations)

For any of the grid systems and mapping / diagramming, consider using the following:

- Local Department of Transportation surveyors (they will most likely have up-to-date equipment and know how to use it)
- Military (check with your nearest director of military support through your incident manager and operations center, and ask for personnel equipped with military GPS)
- Anthropology instructors / senior college students (often, local law enforcement will have an anthropologist on call. If it does not, go through your incident manager and operations center and request that they check local colleges and universities that have anthropology programs.)

Summary

The actions you take during the search and recovery phase of the operational response may set the tone of the entire operation. Mistakes made here often go undiscovered and are perpetuated to the point where they can no longer be corrected. Even if those mistakes are caught early on they can be difficult or impossible to correct.

The search and recovery operations of remains, fragments, and personal effects from a mass fatality incident are not difficult operations if approached from a systematic and thorough way. Establish a logical sequence, ensure everyone follows it, institute a system of checks and balances, and your operation should run very smoothly.

Incident managers should consider a variety of response agencies when deciding who to put on search teams. They should also look at the available technology and how it can be used to better document the site and provide a detailed view of the search and recovery.

Morgue Operations

6

The Mass Fatality Morgue

The mass fatality morgue is the most resource-intensive response location. It is intensive in its manpower requirements, its logistical support requirements, and its emotional toll. It is here that the remains are brought to tell their story. If it is told successfully, they will leave the mass fatality morgue with a confirmed identification. Additionally, readers of the story (incident investigators) will be able to establish the facts surrounding their deaths.

In this chapter we will outline the procedures of establishing, operating, and maintaining a mass fatality incident morgue. In many previous incidents, the morgues were often referred to as "temporary," because they were established only as long as it took to resolve the incident. However, in some mass fatality incidents, the medical examiner's existing facilities are the best available, so they are called the mass fatality incident morgue. So this could be the medical examiner's existing morgue, a morgue established just for the incident, or a combination of both.

Additionally, a morgue is usually a place for medicolegal autopsy and investigation. In most jurisdictions, aftercare such as embalming, restoration, dressing, casketing, or preparation for transport does not routinely occur. However, given that one of the goals in a mass fatality incident is to release the remains as quickly as possible, in the best condition possible, it is often the best choice to have aftercare completed right at the mass fatality incident morgue.

Therefore, when we refer to a mass fatality incident morgue, we mean the facility or facilities where the confirmed identification of the remains is established, where a medicolegal autopsy (if required) is performed, where detailed death incident reports are filled out, and where all elements of aftercare are completed.

Typical mass fatality incident morgues include the following stations

- Administration
- Receiving
- Initial holding
- Photography
- Personal effects
- Fingerprinting or footprinting
- Dental
- Radiology
- Autopsy and inspection
- Anthropology
- Final holding
- aftercare
- Release

Each of these stations may not be required for a particular incident; the order in which the stations are established and their exact layout may be changed so that they are similar, but not exactly alike, during any two incidents. The stations and their setups must be tailored to meet the incident's needs, the available resources, and what the desired outcome is.

Establishment of Morgue Operations

Temporary mass fatality incident morgues have been established in response to a multitude of mass fatality incidents. Large festival or carnival tents, high-school gyms, skating rinks, aircraft hangers, and even churches have served to house these temporary facilities (Figure 6.1).

Following the site assessment, the ME must decide if the mass fatality incident is going to require that a mass fatality incident morgue be set up.

Key factors to consider are:

- The numbers of fatalities and their condition
- The distance from the incident site to a permanent morgue
- The availability of suitable facilities for the establishment of a mass fatality incident morgue
- The ability of the regular morgue to accommodate and expand

(a)

(b)

Figure 6.1 Two mass fatality incident morgues. In (a) tents and screening material have been set up to house a large morgue; (b) shows a local soccer club gymnasium used to house the morgue. Note the crowds gathered around the gym. In areas with limited security, you may have crowds this close to your facility, which will often hamper access. (Courtesy of Kenyon International Emergency Services, Inc.)

- The impact on the ME's normal day-to-day caseload, and whether it will be possible to keep the regular cases separate from the mass fatality incident cases
- Access to equipment necessary to equip a temporary morgue

It will also be imperative to consider what staff will be available, how the operation will be funded, and what the expected end state is.

Response actions by other agencies might occur concurrently with the ME's operations. Other investigators may request that they be given access to the morgue to view and examine the deceased to look for and collect evidence or to take possession of all personal effects. They might also want specific tests conducted on the bodies to look for the presence of particular substances. They will possibly want you to conduct recoveries while they are still in the process of making the scene safe.

If the numbers and conditions of the bodies are such that they will overwhelm the existing morgue, a temporary mass fatality facility should be established as the sole morgue or as a secondary morgue to operate concurrently with the existing one.

If the numbers and conditions of the bodies will not overwhelm the existing morgue or the existing morgue will be used concurrently with the mass fatality one, I recommend the following:

- Establish a separate area for existing cases and new arrivals that are not related to the mass fatality incident.
- Use a system of color coding for all mass fatality incident case files. Thus, if they are accidentally mislaid or filed during the incident response, they are easily identified as belonging to the mass fatality incident.
- Identify one or two staff members to serve as the point of contact for information on existing or new nonincident cases.
- Have prearranged agreements with neighboring buildings and offices for increased parking, security, and many areas that we will discuss later in this chapter. Remember that a mass fatality incident is a very emotional event—if you are involved in the response, most if not all of your focus will be on your job, however, keep in mind that it will end and things will return to normal. Expanding your operation without advising or setting up working agreements with agencies that work closely with you in your regular day-to-day activities, but are not involved in the mass fatality incident response, can jeopardize your future working relationships.

Facility Considerations

Once the medical examiner has made the decision to establish a mass fatality morgue, the next thing to decide is where. Considerations for this are:

- Is there a suitable location close to the incident site?
- Does the facility support compliance with all OSHA regulations?
- Does it have controlled access, to keep the public—specifically photographers—back, but still allow access for removal vehicles and responders?
- Does the facility have the basics such as water, and sewer? If those are present, can electricity and climate control be supplied through the use of auxiliary support items?

Ideally, as part of pre-incident planning, suitable central locations will have been previously identified. If that has not happened it must be done now. Ensure that you look for facilities that have the following, in order of priority:

- Proximity to the incident site, but not so close as to impede rescue operations or be in danger from secondary building collapse, explosions, or other problems
- Sufficient space to accommodate the morgue stations
- Single story or, if more than one story, having a heavy hydraulic lift
- Good ventilation and lighting
- Ability to easily accommodate morgue vehicles, refrigeration vans, and service vehicles
- Established electricity, water, and waste and water disposal, or the ability to easily receive those services through auxiliary means
- Easily cleaned surfaces to meet OSHA or similar requirements

The decision on what facility to use must often be made rapidly. Immediately following the decision, the establishment of the mass fatality incident morgue must begin.

Establishment of Morgue Stations

Receiving

The receiving station is the first place that remains are brought to at the mass fatality incident morgue, and all must go through the receiving station, whose primary functions and flow are:

1. Receive the remains or personal effects

When the remains arrive at the receiving station the following actions take place:

- The case number painted on the human-remains pouch is checked against the number on the tag attached to the remains or fragments.
- The arrival time and case number is noted on a log, which is a chronological record noting the time remains or fragments arrive at the receiving station and when they are moved to other morgue stations.

The remains are checked and the following key points are noted.

- Are the remains currently viewable or can restorative work make them so?
- What type of postmortem identification procedures can be done? In other words, are there printable fingers, is there any dentition, or will X-rays and DNA testing most likely be required? Conducting a quick external examination will help facilitate the procedure. For example, if there are no printable fingers, the remains or fragment can skip the fingerprint station and perhaps go right to the dental station.

In this role, the receiving station can help program and ensure a smooth flow of operations that best utilizes the available resources.

2. Initiate case file folder

A case file is initiated. The case file is a simple folder that should be large enough to hold any documentation that will be created at the morgue. At a minimum, the case file folder should have

- The case number printed neatly and legibly on the outside.

- A printed checklist that includes each station and the forms used at that station. As stations are completed, notes can be made on the checklist. When the case file folder is reviewed for quality control, it is easy to verify that all the required documents are present.

- A log showing dates as well as start and completion times for any actions involving particular remains.

The case file folder is then placed in a file stand or holder where it is easy to retrieve when a escort comes to get the body or fragment.

3. Place remains in temporary refrigerated holding or assign an escort. If morgue operations have all stations fully operational, not overloaded, and capable of receiving remains, they should be assigned an escort and moved to the appropriate station.

If, however, the morgue is not yet fully established, is currently working at full capacity, or if escorts are unavailable, the body or fragment should be immediately placed into the refrigeration van or unit.

It should be the responsibility of the receiving station to ensure that the refrigeration van or unit is maintained at the proper temperature. It should be checked hourly. If it is a portable unit, receiving station personnel should ensure that all required services and deliveries of fuel (if required) are made.

A note of caution, if pre-incident plans call for the making and installation of a racking system to be placed into refrigerated vans that will serve as temporary holding units, ensure that you do not overload the refrigeration system. A uniform temperature should be maintained, and that can be difficult with a large number of remains.

Additionally, ensure that no commercial logos or company names are visible on the refrigeration trailers (Figures 6.2 and 6.2a).

Figure 6.2 Commercial refrigeration vehicles used at a mass fatality incident morgue. Note that all commercial markings have been removed. (Courtesy of Kenyon International Emergency Services, Inc.)

4. Assign escorts
Once a body or fragment has begun movement through the mass fatality incident morgue, it should always be with an escort. The escort is responsible for ensuring that:

- The remains are not mixed up or commingled with any other remains

Figure 6.2a A typical mass fatality incident morgue interior area. (Courtesy of Kenyon International Emergency Services, Inc.)

- The case file folder and finished documents are complete
- The case file is turned in to the administration station
- The proper dignity and respect is paid to the remains at all times

5. Update status board
The status board maintained by the administration station should be updated to reflect the arrival of the remains or fragments to the mass fatality incident morgue.

Administration

The administration station serves as the brain and nerve center of the mass fatality incident morgue. In some operations, it is called a morgue operations center. Its primary functions are:

1. Collects and collates all known antemortem identification records
As points of contact, such as family dentists or doctors, military records, and other antemortem information is gathered from the family assistance center or the emergency inquiry centers, it is passed to the morgue administration center.

Here personnel will collect the information from the points of contact. A large wall chart should be used to note ongoing antemortem record-collection status.

Information will likely come from many sources and may involve law enforcement officers visiting homes to collect fingerprints and hair samples. Additionally, surviving family members may be asked to give blood or tissue sample for DNA comparison. Those results and records should all come to the morgue administration station.

2. Manages or administers case files

As a body or fragment is taken through the morgue process, post-mortem case files are created. These most often consist of various reports and completed forms such as finger- or footprint cards, lab reports, detailed dental, anthropological or pathology diagrams, photographs, written reports, and most importantly, confirmed identification. When these records are not being reviewed, they should be kept at the morgue administration station. Any time the records are removed they should be signed out and a sign-out card placed in the file.

At the conclusion of the incident response, the case files should be filed in accordance with local laws and customs for death records.

3. Acts as single point of contact (POC) for all morgue operations

Any request for information should be passed to and answered by the administration station. Please note, as discussed in Chapter 9, media inquiries should always be answered by trained spokespersons. However, inquiries from family members or other response agencies should be directed to the administration station, which, as organized, should always have the most current and complete information. Therefore, to avoid answering questions twice, a single POC should be established.

The administration station also serves to coordinate work shifts, and the procurement and maintenance of equipment and supplies.

4. Monitors status board

A simple status board should be established at the onset of an incident and maintained throughout the incident. In large incidents, when a temporary morgue is used as well as an existing morgue, a computerized status board should be used so entries can be visible by both morgues. Status boards are very simple, often created with spreadsheets or, more often, drawn on bristol board and tacked to a large open area. A sample status board is shown in Figure 6.3.

The administration station personnel should update the status board any time a change is made to the status of the remains or fragments.

INCIDENT _____

MASS FATALITY INCIDENT MORGUE STATUS BOARD

DATE OF INCIDENT _____

Case Number	Identification Last, First, MI	Administration Station		Receiving Station		Initial Holding Station		Photography Station		Personal Effects Station	
		Date	Time	Date	Time	Date	Time	Date	Time	Date	Time

Figure 6.3   Suggested mass fatality incident morgue status board.

Finger / Foot Print Station		Dental Station		Radiology Station		Autospy Station		Anthropolgy Station		Final Holding Station		After Care Station	
Date	Time	Date	Time	Date	Time	Date	Time	Date	Time	Date	Time	Date	Time

Figure 6.3 Continued

MASS FATALITY INCIDENT MORGUE STATUS BOARD

Release Station			Remarks
Date	Time	Reciver	

Figure 6.3 Continued

Photography

The photography station serves to document the initial condition of the remains. Additional close-up photography may be required at other morgue stations. The station's primary functions and flow are:

1. **Photographing the remains**
   - Ensure that the case number is included in every photograph.
   - Assign skilled forensic photographers. There will not be a second chance to take pictures.
   - Photographs should taken with both color and black-and-white film.
   - Stepladders or a platform should be provided for overhead photographs.
   - No objects should be removed from the remains. Specific detailed close-ups will most likely be required at other stations.
   - Enough forensic photographs should be present to provide support to other stations as required.

A note of caution, assigned photographers should be the only people with cameras or photographic equipment in the entire mass fatality incident morgue. Several states have introduced legislation that required agencies to ensure that pictures and film from crime scenes and other scenes are used for official use only. The intent of the legislation is to establish penalties for those who pass such photographs to the media. Additionally, professional responders who sometime take photographs and later use them in teaching or scientific presentations would need a signed release from the next of kin of each person shown in a photograph.

Clearly, the safest route is to allow no cameras or photographic equipment for anyone but specific designated photographers. You still must be cautious; in one particularly noteworthy case, inappropriate images were linked to the media or placed on the Internet causing additional trauma to the victim's family. The bottom line—no scrapbook photos should be taken.

2. **Updating the status board**
After the photographs are taken the status should be updated to reflect this.

3. **Updating the case file**
Escort notes completion of initial photography on case file folder checklist. They should then note in the log:

- The name(s) of photographers
- The number of photographs taken
- The date and time photography was completed

Initial Inspection and Removal of Personal Effects

In this station, the remains are inspected for obvious items of value, and the personal effects, including clothing, is removed. It is important that these things are accomplished early on. Trace evidence can be lost or contaminated if it reacts with chemicals normally found in the mass fatality incident morgue. Personal effects may become lost or receive further damage if not immediately protected.

　　1.　Remove the remains from the human-remains pouch.
The body or fragments should be removed from the human-remains pouch and placed onto a clean gurney. The pouch should be disposed of as contaminated waste.

　　Ensure that you thoroughly inspect the human-remains pouch for any personal effects, potential evidence items, or tissue that may have separated from the remains during movement.

　　2.　Remove, inspect, and document personal effects.
After you have removed the remains from the human-remains pouch you should now carefully remove all visible personal effects.

　　Remove each item and place into a separate plastic bag.

　　As each item is removed, a narrative description should be placed on an inventory form. Inventories should reflect generic terms such as

- "Yellow colored metal" for items believed to be made of gold
- "Silver colored metal" for items believed to be made from silver or platinum
- "Clear stone like" for items believed to be diamonds
- "Colored stone like" for items believed to be other precious gems
- Watch, with name "Rolex" (as opposed to Rolex watch)

Although writing inventories in such a manner is time consuming, it is the best way to protect your agency and yourself. As remote as it may seem, some next of kin will demand a diamond ring if an inventory noted a diamond ring, even if the item was clearly costume jewelry.

　　Ensure that all areas are checked for jewelry items; it is not uncommon to find ankle bracelets, wristbands, tongue studs, and other types of body jewelry and body piercing on victims.

　　As each item is removed, it should also be checked for any identification value; rings, bracelets, and necklaces often have unique inscriptions. Class rings are also useful. When any item is found that could have potential identification value, that information should be noted as part of the inventory form and also a special notation should be made on the case file folder checklist. Additionally, an instant photo of the item should be taken and placed into the case file, so that it may be shown to families to see if they recognize it, which may again help with the establishment of a confirmed identification.

Once all visible items have been removed and placed into separate marked plastic bags, these bags should then be placed in a large clear plastic bag, with the case number clearly written on the outside. This bag always stays with the remains. It is never separated while in the mass fatality morgue.

If any item is removed by law enforcement or other investigative agents, a description of the item being removed, the name of the person removing the items, the agency the person represents and the date and time of removal should be noted in the case log (Figure 6.4).

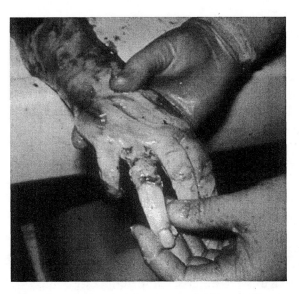

Figure 6.4 Inspection of remains for personal effects. (Courtesy of Kenyon International Emergency Services, Inc.)

3. **Remove, inspect, and document clothing**
   - After all the visible personal effects have been removed, inventoried, and placed into bags, all clothing items should be removed. Care should be taken to do no further damage to the clothing.
   - The clothing should also be inspected for personal effects that may have been missed earlier, as well as any tags or markings that could aid with establishing a tentative identification.
   - The clothing items should be inventoried.

- Clothing should be placed into paper bags, with the case number written clearly on the outside of the bag.
- The bag should stay with the remains or fragments at all times.

4. Update the status board.

After the initial survey and removal and documentation of personal effects and clothing is complete the status should be updated to reflect this.

5. Update the case file.

The escort should note in the case file folder checklist the completion of this station's requirements. They should ensure that all actions taken, to include the removal of any items, and items noted for possible identification value have all been noted in the log.

Finger- or Footprinting

The finger- or footprint section is the first section where a confirmed identification can be established. All remains with printable fingers should be fingerprinted. Additionally, bodies without printable fingers should have footprints and palm prints taken.

Although many local jurisdictions in the U.S. have outstanding criminalists who are experts at taking fingerprints, consideration should be given to using the Federal Bureau of Investigation's (FBI) disaster identification team. Its members are available free to any jurisdiction and can be requested through your local FBI office. They have been involved in many disasters over the last several years.

The decision as to whether a finger is printable should be left up to the fingerprint experts. Many times they are able to get prints from remains that most thought were impossible. In some cases, fingers bearing visible ridge detail cannot be adequately printed, but experts can remove the skin and photograph the ridge detail, which can later be compared with known prints.

If the finger(s) and or hand(s) have been amputated at the morgue, they should be placed in a receptacle that contains the original case number and a notation that they were amputated at the morgue, and were not separate fragment(s) recovered independently of any remains. Furthermore, the receptacle and its contents should never be moved to an area away from the remains. In other words, if a criminalist is examining the finger(s) and or hand(s), the donor remains and the accompanying escort should be close by.

1. Print Fingers or Foot

The remains should be moved to the finger- or footprinting station. Here the criminalist should take prints from finger(s), palm(s), and feet as needed.

If it becomes necessary to amputate fingers or hand, this should be done here. However, this should be done only as a matter of necessity and not just for a matter of convenience. Once the finger(s) or hand is removed, it could be lost or inadvertently associated with another body. Additionally, if the body is viewable, the amputated finger(s) or hand(s) may cause additional trauma to the family. The decision-making authority for this should be the medical examiner (Figure 6.5).

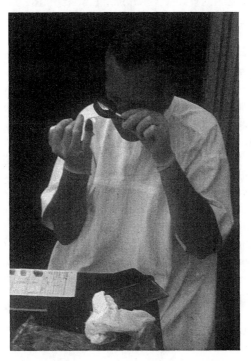

Figure 6.5 A forensic expert places a portion of skin removed from a victim over his gloved finger to allow for better examination. (Courtesy of Kenyon International Emergency Services, Inc.)

2. Update the status board.

After any prints are taken the status board should be updated to reflect this.

3. Update case file

The escort should note in the case file folder checklist the completion of this station, ensuring that all actions taken are noted on the log.

They should then note in the log:
1. The name(s) of criminalist(s)
2. Approval of, and subsequent amputation of, finger(s) and hand(s), to include approval authority
3. The number and type of prints made
4. The date and time printing was completed

X-ray Station

The X-ray station serves several purposes. Potential uses for full-body X-rays are to:

- Reveal documented antemortem artifacts that are useful in establishing a confirmed identification.
- Reveal foreign objects in remains. These objects can be personal effects, evidence, and, in cases of explosives, hazardous explosive components.
- Reveal teeth in an otherwise indistinguishable mass of human tissue and bone (Figures 6.6 and 6.7).

Therefore, all remains or fragments should be X-rayed as part of the medicolegal procedure.

1. Take X-ray.
The escort should take the remains to the X-ray station, where a qualified trained X-ray technician will take a complete full body X-ray. The X-ray should be developed and checked to ensure that it is readable and clear prior to the remains' being taken from this station.

Once the X-ray is complete and the film developed and checked, the escort should place the developed file into the case file.

2. Update status board.
After the X-rays are taken the status board should be updated to reflect this.

3. Update case file.
The escort should note in the case file folder checklist the completion of this station, and ensure that all actions taken have been noted in the log.

They should then note in the log:

- The name(s) of X-ray technician(s)
- The number of X-rays made
- The date and time X-rays were completed

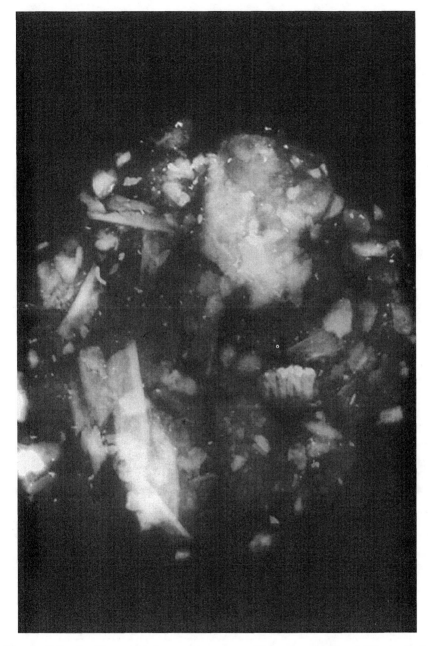

Figure 6.6 An X-ray of a large tissue mass. Note the clearly visible teeth in the right center. Without X-ray, these teeth might not have been found, and positive identification of the victim might not have been made. (Courtesy of Dr. Faruk Presswalla, New Jersey Medical Examiner.)

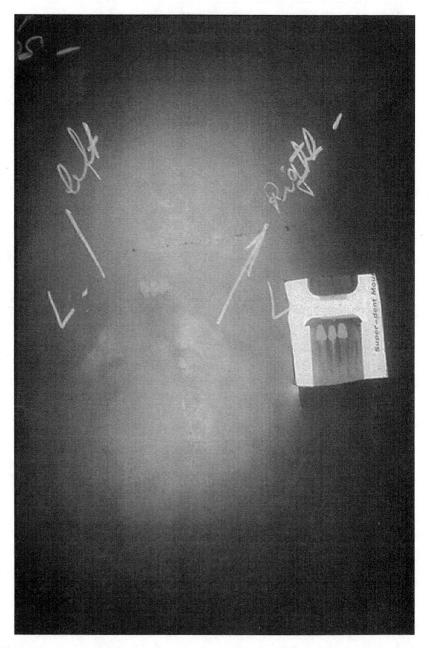

Figure 6.7 X-ray of a large tissue mass showing visible teeth and the inserted antemortem X-ray of the same teeth, which was used to establish identification. (Courtesy of Dr. Faruk Presswalla, New Jersey Medical Examiner.)

Dental Station

More people have dental X-rays on file than have fingerprint records on file. Therefore, a confirmed identification through the comparison of antemortem and post-mortem dental records is often the most-used method for establishing a confirmed identification of mass fatality incident victims. Additionally, new methods have been tested and are now used whereby DNA is extracted from a single tooth. The DNA can then be matched against donor samples to establish a confirmed identification.

In fact, because of the use of dentition in confirming identification, dental organizations have often led the way in establishing local mass fatality incident response teams and procedures.

All remains with any dentition whatsoever should go through the dental station.

A note on facial dissection or jaw resection, just as in the decision to amputate fingers, the decision to partially dissect the face or do a jaw resection must be based on necessity and not convenience. The approval authority for facial dissection or jaw resection should be only the medical examiner.

If jaw resection is approved, the resection should be accomplished using a Stryker autopsy saw, chisel and mallet, or other cutting device and not by means of disarticulation at the temporomandibular joints. This is done in case a question arises as to what remains the resected jaw belongs with. Comparisons of the cut can establish which resected jaw belongs to which remains.

An additional area of concern is that the resected jaw should only leave the mass fatality incident morgue after it has been returned to the donor remains. This is done so that resected jaws are not lost or unintentionally destroyed.

A resected jaw should be placed in a receptacle that contains the original case number and a notation that the jaw was resected and not a separate fragment recovered independently of any remains. Furthermore, the receptacle and resected jaw should never be removed to a different area from the remains. In other words, if a forensic odontologist is examining the jaw, its remains and accompanying escort should be close by.

1. **Dentagram is done of all deceased.**
The escort should move the remains to the dental station.

A forensic odontologist should then make the determination as to what actions will occur. All or any of the following actions may occur, based on the decision of the forensic odontologist:

Complete dental charting, which includes:

•. Record of all teeth, charted using the universal tooth numbering system and the name of the tooth.
•. Missing teeth, caries, and fractures should be noted.
•. All restorative work should be noted, and completely described.

Complete dental X-rays should be taken. Just as with a full-body X-ray, the remains should not leave the dental station until the X-rays are developed and checked for accuracy and clarity. Intra-oral photographs should also be taken (Figure 6.8).

Figure 6.8 Jaw fragment with an identifying tag. (Courtesy of Kenyon International Emergency Services, Inc.)

2. Update Status Board
After the dental examination is complete, the status board should be updated to reflect this.

3. Update case file
The escort should note in the case file folder checklist the completion of this station, ensuring that all actions taken have been noted in the log.
They should then note in the log:

• The name(s) of forensic odontologist, dental assistants, photographers, and X-ray technicians who examined the remains
• Approval of, and subsequent facial dissections or jaw resection, to include approval authority
• The number of X-rays made

- The date and time X-rays were completed

Anthropology

Forensic anthropologists have played a key role in many death investigations and in mass fatality incidents. In fact, in the U.S., the National Transportation Safety Board now has a Forensic Anthropologist as one of its full time investigators. Forensic Anthropologist can do several things at an incident site. In conjunction with other specialist forensic anthropologists can help distinguish human from non-human remains, many recent incidents have involved the recovery of small skeletal structures that most people thought were children, when in fact the structures turned out to be the remains of small animals.

In addition to the above forensic anthropologists can also help determine:

1. Number of fatalities
2. Gender of victims
3. Age of victims
4. Race of victims

Forensic anthropologists will also be able to observe and comment on:

1. Anomalies or individualizing traits
2. Antemortem, perimortem, and postmortem trauma
3. Antemortem and postmortem radiographic comparison

1. Forensic Anthropologist Examination

Prior to the escort bringing the remains to the forensic anthropologist, the remains should have already been X-rayed. The forensic anthropologist will then examine the remains and create their reports based on their findings, in some cases maceration, or removal of all soft tissue from the bones must occur. In these cases the forensic anthropologist should consult the medical examiner who should be the final authority. As in other procedures that change or alter the structure of the remains, care should be taken to document all actions. Additionally, the remains should not be moved from the mass fatality incident morgue, where any maceration should be accomplished.

2. Update Status Board

After the anthropological examination is complete the status board should be updated to reflect this.

3. Update Case File

The escort should note in the case file folder checklist the completion of this station, they should ensure that all actions taken have been noted on the log
    They should then note in the log:

1. 1. The names of forensic anthropologists, photographers, and X-ray technicians who examined the remains
2. Approval of, and subsequent maceration, to include approval authority
3. The number of X-rays made
4. The date and time X-rays were completed

Medicolegal Autopsy

As was discussed in the beginning of this chapter and to a lesser extent in the beginning of this guide, the medical examiner must make the determination on how many, if any and to what extent any medicolegal autopsies will be completed. There is no pat answer to this.

On one hand, some will suggest that the medical examiner should consider the type of incident, the number and condition of remains, and the wishes of the families. However, with today's society being as litigious as it is, even natural disasters can result in litigation where demonstrated pain and suffering can result in additional monetary awards for family members. Additionally, family members often, not always, but often will eventually want to know exactly what happened to their loved one. Even cases that appear straightforward at the outset may in fact present problems at a later date. Therefore, I recommend that all remains undergo a medicolegal autopsy.

If the decision is made not to conduct complete medicolegal autopsies, in the case of certain transportation accidents I do recommend that the medical examiner check with the authorities investigating the incident to determine if other laws or regulations require the medicolegal autopsy of certain crew members or equipment operators.

I further recommend that from the initial response to the incident the medical examiner make it clear of the intention to complete medicolegal autopsy and solicit the support of a variety of local religious leaders. Clearly, most laws give the medical examiner the jurisdiction to determine when an autopsy will be performed and the option to perform one, even if it is against the wishes of the family. However, medical examiners should be sensitive to the need of the family and try to reach a balance.

Once the medical examiner has decided what, if any level of a medicolegal autopsy is to be performed they must then determine how many autopsy stations to set up and how many forensic pathologist will be needed to adequately staff the stations.

In chapters four and six, of the Forensic Science Foundation's *Medicolegal Death Investigations, Treatises in the Forensic Sciences*, has established and published some basic guidelines for the type of, and amount of reference tissue and fluid specimens that should be collected and recommended methods for their preservation. I suggest that the medical examiner follow those recommendations. Because they are readily available in those publications, I will not repeat them here. Any reference samples that are taken should be clearly labeled and remain at the mass fatality incident morgue until the mass fatality incident morgue is closed. At that time the reference samples should be moved to the medical examiners normal storage location. They should not be destroyed until such time as allowed by statue or when all litigation is completed, whichever is later.

If a medicolegal autopsy is not performed, the forensic pathologist should at least view and inspect all remains. The depth of the inspection should be sufficient to review and concur with any diagramming and charting the autopsy assistants have completed. The forensic pathologist should ensure that they are comfortable in signing the death certificate and, if required, being able to stand in court and answer all relevant questions relating to the cause, manner, mechanism, pain and suffering, and conditions surrounding the death of each individual victim. In cases where one or more of those questions cannot be answered, the only acceptable reason should be because the scientific technology for us to make a determination does not yet exist. The unacceptable answer is I do not know because I did not conduct the proper examination, test, or keep accurate and detailed records.

Flow

The medical examiner should use whatever systematic flow they are comfortable with. Whatever system you use it should include the following steps:

1. Weigh the remains
2. Complete detailed diagram of injury patterns, missing portions, and any other artifacts as required
3. Take any additional photographs that have not already been taken
4. Review the work such as X-rays, anthropological examinations, and dental charting that was completed at earlier stations
5. Take any external fluid samples
6. Complete any invasive procedures, to include collection and examination of fluids and tissue samples, that are going to be done
7. After the medicolegal autopsy or inspection is complete, the forensic pathologist, in conjunction with forensic odontologist, forensic

anthropologist, radiologist, and criminalist should make a determination and arrive to decision as the confirmed identification of a deceased.

Easy enough statement to make, but it can be and is often a difficult challenge to execute. Let's take a minute to look at the flow of the event. If the mass fatality incident is properly managed, as the mass fatality morgue is being established, the remains are being recovered, and family assistance personnel are, along with criminalist and other specialists, collecting antemortem identification records. Those records should be then centralized in the mass fatality morgue administration station. Once the records start to arrive there are a variety of ways to collate and organize them.

The antemortem records can be hand sorted by certain categories such as gender, race, age, and stature. Or the information from the records can be entered into one of the many computer-aided identification programs that exist such as Computer Aided Postmortem Identification (CAPMI) or Windows Identification (WinID). The Skeltrak System™, a brand new death investigation management system promises to greatly assist in the management of identification processing. It was developed by a death investigator and is currently being sold through Skeltrak™ Systems in Sarasota, Florida.

Concurrent to this, as remains pass through the various mass fatality incident morgue stations, antemortem records are being created. Therefore, these records also have to be sorted and organized. If you are using computer-aided programs, then the data must also be entered in the computer databank. Programs such as CAMPI, WinID, and Skeltrak™ can be of great assistance, if you have the trained personnel and required computer equipment (a desktop or laptop computer, monitor, and printer.) The various programs work by comparing all postmortem records against the information that is entered into the antemortem section. As the computer compares records, possible matches are generated. Just as with the Automated Fingerprint Identification System (AFIS), the postmortem and antemortem data are converted in a series of markers that are compared with each other. The program looks for a certain number of matches, and when that number is reached, generates a possible match. Once the possible matches are generated the actual postmortem and antemortem records should then be compared by the various forensic disciplines to establish a confirmed identification.

Regardless of the method used, the medical examiner should use his consulting or supporting experts and make a determination; in some cases, the decision will have to wait pending more detailed lab work and study. And as discussed in the glossary, exclusion may be a method of last result.

Clearly, the establishment of positive identification will start out by going from easiest to hardest, in other words the remains that are easy to identify will be identified first. Then as the number of as yet to be identified victims is reduced, so is list of the missing and the amount of postmortem records to be checked.

If the confirmed identification cannot easily be established through finger or foot or palm printing, or dental identification, then the other methods as previously described should be used. Remember that the accompanying personal effects are still with the remains and may yield clues that can lead to establishing a positive identification. Additionally, multiple methods should be used. A case in point, DNA sample taken from a remains or fragment may actually belong to another remains or fragment. In some high-impact incidents, blood and body tissue from one victim may be deposited onto another victim. If only one sample is taken from remains it might just be the blood or tissue that was deposited by another victim.

Once the confirmed identification is completed the death certificate should also be completed, which at a minimum should include the cause, manner, and mechanism of death.

Additionally, once the confirmed identification is established, the surviving family members should be immediately notified. Trained personnel, in a private setting should conduct notification face to face.

Author's note: Care should be taken to ensure that the process of completing the actual death certificate form is done as soon as possible. The reason for this is simple; in addition to the emotional trauma that a mass fatality incident produces, there is the very real and practical problem of financial support to the surviving families. Unfortunately, today many people live month to month with no emergency cushion, and when a primary wage earner or even a supporting wage earner dies in a mass fatality incident, their income stops. In some cases, such as aviation accidents, temporary emergency funding is provided to the families, but that may not always be the case. Therefore the bulk of surviving families depend on the life insurance proceeds to get by. However, most life insurance policies will not pay out until a death certificate has been issued. In recent incidents it has taken months for death certificates to be issued and made available to the surviving families.

Many people think that if a person was in a building that collapsed or on a plane that crashed, and any survivors have been accounted for, that the families already know that their loved ones have died. However, that for many families is not reality. People generally want to hold out and hope for the best. In some cases, victims have survived days trapped in collapsed buildings when most hope is gone. In some plane crashes, most notably, a recent one in Detroit, everyone on board a large aircraft, with the exception of one small child, was killed. It was truly a miracle that the child survived, so miracles do happen. Therefore, until the families are told that a confirmed identification has been made, they may continue to hold out hope for the survival of their loved one.

8. Place the Remains into Human-Remains Pouches

Once the medicolegal autopsy or inspection is complete, the remains should be placed in a new human-remains pouch. The pouch should still be heavy duty, a different color from those used for recovery (to ensure that remains that have gone through the morgue stations are not accidentally placed with remains that are just being brought in.) A tag with the case file number should be attached to the remains, and another tag attached to the human-remains pouch, as well as the case number being painted on the human-remains pouch. The escort should return the remains to the final holding area.

9. Move Personal Effects to Personal Effects Warehouse or Operational Area

After a the medical examiner has completed the medicolegal autopsy of inspection, accompanying personal effects, if any, should be transported to the personal effects warehouse, if established, or other personal effects operational area. Although, in most jurisdictions the daily operational method is for the personal effects to be released directly to the family or with the remains or fragments, I recommend that this not be the case here.

This recommendation is because the majority of mass fatality incidents involving severe trauma to the remains, which cause the personal effects to be damaged and soiled with bodily fluids. Additionally, the sheer scope and scale of mass fatality incidents requires that, just as extra procedures are in place for the care of victims, so must they be in place for personal effects.

The accompanying personal effects should then be turned over to the representatives of the personal effects warehouse or operations. A joint inventory is should be conducted and any discrepancies resolved before either the receiving or transferring personal go on to any other actions.

10. Update Status Board

After the medicolegal autopsy or inspections is complete the status board should be updated to reflect this. Once the confirmed identification is established the status board should also reflect this.

11. Update Case File

The escort should note in the case file folder checklist the completion of this station, and should ensure that all actions taken have been noted on the log.
    They should then note in the log:

1. The names of forensic pathologist and any other specialists who assisted in the medicolegal autopsy of death investigation.
2. The name(s) of the person accepting custody of the personal effects and a copy of the signed joint inventory.

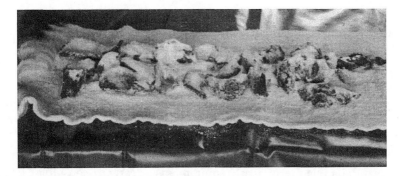

Figure 6.9 Embalming powder being applied to various fragments. Here, sanitation and preservation are not for viewing, but to preserve the fragments for later interment. (Courtesy of Kenyon International Emergency Services, Inc.)

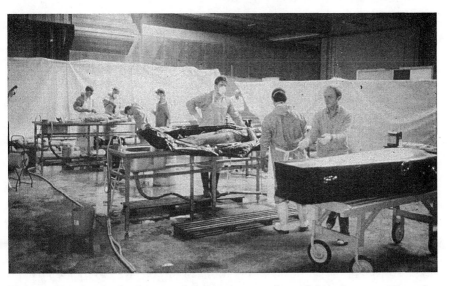

Figure 6.10 Mass fatality incident morgue configured for aftercare. Note the screening of the aftercare station, which is used to reduce workers' exposure to the deceased. (Courtesy of Kenyon International Emergency Services, Inc.)

Aftercare

Aftercare is defined as those sanitation, preservation, and restorations services that may be required by law or desired by the families. In most cases the services involve embalming or the application of other means of preservation, restorative cosmetology to enhance or make viewing of the remains possible, preparation for transportation, often across jurisdictional boundaries, and casketing (Figures 6.9 and 6.10)

Quite normally, aftercare services are performed away from the morgue and usually accomplished in a mortuary. However, because of the scope of a mass fatality incident it might be better to include aftercare services as part of the morgue stations. Factors to consider are:

Location of the mass fatality incident morgue in relation to local mortuaries; in other words, are there enough local mortuaries in close proximity to handle the remains in a timely manner? Remember, the goal is to release the remains to the families for final disposition as soon as possible.

The structure of the mass fatality incident morgue, is it large enough and equipped to handle the aftercare requirements. Clearly, an ideal mass fatality incident morgue should be capable of supporting all possible requirements, however, many mass fatality incidents rarely happen in ideal locations, so consideration must be given to the most important tasks, such as medicolegal death investigation and then aftercare.

Consider the legal requirements if an incident occurs in an area far removed from the final disposition location and many of the remains will have to cross jurisdictional boundaries prior to arriving at that location. In such a case, it would probably be best to include aftercare as part of the mass fatality morgue.

Another issue is the cost of adding aftercare to the morgue. In most jurisdictions, it is the responsibility of the governmental to pay for the costs associated with the medicolegal death investigation. However, it is the responsibility of the families or third parties to pay for the costs of aftercare. Therefore, depending on the incident, the agreement on who pays for what should be decided upon prior to the decision on what services are provided for. This is not said to be insensitive, it is the responsibility of the local government officials (medical examiner) to preserve their resources and ensure that they serve diligently the people who appoint or elect them.

If the length of time for recovery and identification operations is going to be considerable, serious consideration should be given to including some aftercare (preservation). For example, if the recovery of remains and subsequent procedures to establish confirmed identification are going to take several weeks or even months, then remains that have completed the medicolegal autopsy should be have action taken for sanitation and preservation.

In addition to these factors, care should be given to the families' desires. There are many different customs and rules for the aftercare of the deceased, each different and based on the individual religious beliefs and desires. In some cases such as the transportation of remains across jurisdictional boundaries, embalming will be required before the remains can be moved from the local area. Again, the support of local religious leaders can make the medical examiner's job easier.

If the medical examiner makes the decision to include aftercare as part of the morgue operation, than several aftercare stations should be set-up in the morgue. Again because aftercare may not be a legal necessity some extra precautions and procedures should be employed.

To begin with, no remains should be given any aftercare until identification has been confirmed and the person authorized to direct disposition has been determined. Unless, of course, the actual or anticipated length of time for completing the confirmed identification or location of the person authorized to direct disposition is such that sanitation and preservation should be accomplished.

Once the confirmed identification and the person authorized to direct disposition has been determined and located and permission given, then whatever aftercare is desired or required should be completed.

In no case should cremation occur in a mass fatality incident morgue. Because the finality of cremation, it should occur only after the remains or fragments have been released form the mass fatality incident morgue custody and care of those remains turned over to those persons authorized to direct disposition.

After this station the remains should removed to the final holding area.

1. Update Status Board

After the aftercare is complete the status board should be updated to reflect this.

2. Update Case File

The escort should note in the case file folder checklist the completion of this station, they should ensure that all actions taken have been noted on the log
    They should then note in the log:

1. The name(s) of funeral directors involved in the aftercare.
2. What aftercare was completed, and, in the case of using chemical sanitation and preservation, the amount and types of chemicals used.

Final Holding Area

This is a separate area to hold remains or fragments until such time as they are released for transportation to an area for final disposition. At this station remains are held in refrigeration or in caskets or shipping containers (Figures 6.11 and 6.12).

This area should be completely separate from the initial holding area.

Figure 6.11   The final stages of typical aftercare area in a mass fatality incident morgue. Many deceased have been placed into coffins. More coffins are awaiting additional remains. (Courtesy of Kenyon International Emergency Services, Inc.)

Once placed into this area all case files should be returned to administration section and only the case file number on the human-remains pouch or tag attached to the casket or shipping container should stay with the remains.

Update Status Board

When the aftercare is completed, the status board should be updated.

Release Area

This is the final mass fatality incident morgue station. Not only should it be the last station in the flow of operations, it should be the only physical location for remains to leave the mass fatality incident morgue.

Keep in mind that, based on the type of incident, it is very probable that multiple fragments will continue to be recovered over a long period of time. As soon as possible, those family members or other persons authorized to direct disposition should be contacted and told that, in some cases, multiple recoveries of fragments of the person with whom they are connected may be recovered and a decision should be reached as to when they would like the body or fragments released. In some cases, they may want the victim released as soon as a confirmed identification is established or they may want the ME to wait and release the remains when it is highly unlikely any other fragments will be recovered.

Once the final disposition instructions are received at the administration station, the administration station should ensure that:

Figure 6.12 Coffins are wrapped in protective paper prior to their transportation to the location determined by the person eligible to direct disposition. This is to ensure that the outside of the coffin is not damaged. (Courtesy of Kenyon International Emergency Services, Inc.)

- The case file folder is complete.
- All required actions have been done and are documented.
- The medical examiner has signed the death certificate or a certificate authorizing release of the remains. I recommend that no more than two people be allowed to sign any release documents, and they should be the medical examiner and morgue administrator.
- That the receiving funeral home or other party that is taking custody of the remains is given a specific time to pick them up.
- A written release, along with the case file folder, should then be sent to the release station providing the case file number, the confirmed identification, the name of the receiving funeral home or other party, and the time the remains are to be picked up.
- Once the receiving funeral home arrives to pick up the remains the release station should:

1. Verify the identification of the funeral director or other receiving party.
2. Retrieve the remains or fragments from the final holding area.
3. Verify the case file number on the release documents to the case file number on the human-remains pouch or on the tag attached to the shipping container, or casket.
4. Have a receipt document signed by the receiving funeral director or other party.

The remains should then be turned over to the receiving funeral director or other designated party.

A copy of the release document, signed by the receiving funeral director or other approved party should then be placed in the case file, which is then returned to the administration section. The completed case files should be placed in a separate filing container. The case files should not be moved from the mass fatality incident morgue until the morgue is closed. This ensures that the case file folder will be available for reference during the resolution of the incident.

Update Status Board

After the release is complete, the status board should be updated.

Morgue Resources

A variety of personnel and equipment resources are required to establish, maintain, and operate the mass fatality incident morgue. In this chapter I have listed some of the specialties required such as the medical examiners, forensic pathologists, forensic anthropologists, forensic photographers, criminalist, and forensic odontologist, however, do not forget all the other support staff and specialist that may be required. Additional personnel to consider are:

- Dental assistants
- Military mortuary affairs specialists
- Evidence collection technicians
- X-ray technicians
- Data entry personnel
- Clerks
- Law enforcement
- Crisis counselors (for staff)
- Legal counsel
- Funeral directors
- Interpreters
- Janitorial or maintenance staff

The challenge here is to identify where these personnel will come from. Again, the benefit of preplanning and mutual aid agreements is clearly demonstrated. As part of the planning process, community resources should be identified to provide these resources if they are needed. Consider local technical schools, medical associations, and volunteer associations. The key is to identify and train the personnel before they are needed.

A word of caution: Although plans are great for identifying the available resources, they do not spell out whether those resources will be capable of working in a mass fatality incident morgue. This can be done to some extent by having programs that gradually exposure these people to regular morgue operations through training and scheduled morgue rotations. This is a lesson we do not seem to learn, yet it could be easily taken care of.

A final thought on staffing a mass fatality incident morgue: Do not use any person under the age of 18; ask for volunteers, but ensure that they are professionals and not people "off the street." There is no room for mistakes, and the cost and risk are too high for the workers.

Summary

From the standpoint of resource requirements the establishment, operation, and maintenance of the mass fatality incident morgue is one of the costliest. It is also one of the most misunderstood and politicized aspects of the entire response operation.

Clearly, however the operation can be managed and effectively organized if approached in a systematic and through way. Establish a logical sequence, ensure everyone follows it, establish a system of checks and balances, and your operation should run very smoothly. Remember to identify key people in your plans and more importantly to train those personnel and gradually expose them to working around remains or fragments. Finally, look at the available technology and how it can be used to better facilitate mass fatality morgue operations.

Personal Effects Operations

7

For the purposes of this guide, "personal effects" (PE) refers to those items carried by, or being transported with, an individual on a common carrier. In mass disasters, the incident scene can be littered with thousands of personal effects. The intent of this guide is to suggest an effective way of properly handling those effects recovered from a definable area unique to that incident.

In a mass fatality incident personal effects take on added meaning. In many cases where natural causes are involved, death is delayed long enough for good-byes to be said. Even when the death occurs suddenly, the family usually has the option of viewing their relative and at least knowing the immediate events surrounding the death incident.

Unfortunately, in a mass fatality incident, death is usually sudden, unexpected, and very violent. More often than not, remains are not viewable — in some cases, very few fragments are recovered and therefore very little can be returned to the family. Additionally, the details of the last few minutes or moments of the victim's life may not be known. Herein lies the significance of the personal effects. They are the only tangible items that are returned to friends or families to represent their loved ones. They are the items that last touched the individual; they are the personal things that often have little monetary value but are priceless to the families. In a sense, they represent the life that has been taken.

It is that very representation that also makes working with personal effects one of the most difficult aspects for responders to work with. As the responders lay out, inventory, clean, and package the personal effects for shipment they discover that they are not just personal effects but a representation of life (Figure 7.1). Each family photograph, stuffed animal, backpack, and piece of jewelry is poignant, evoking an easily imagined history, and the knowledge of a life lost.

Figure 7.1 Responders examining personal effects that have been collected and laid out in a warehouse to dry. (Courtesy Kenyon International Emergency Services, Inc.)

Author's note: Following an incident in which a military person was murdered, I recovered a skill badge that she was wearing at the time of her death. It would have been very easy for the military to provide a replacement badge to the soldier's family, but it would not have been the same. I and other responders involved took extreme care to ensure that the badge recovered on the soldier's body was the one presented to the family. The significance to them was not lost and will probably never be forgotten by her children.

The responsibility for the search, recovery, care, and disposition of personal effects varies among the types of incidents and the jurisdiction in which the incident occurs. There are, however, some basic tenets:

- In many mass fatality incidents personal effects of the deceased and survivors will be recovered and require disposition.
- During ordinary events, or in mass fatality incidents in which only government agencies are responding, personal effects recovered on a body become the responsibility of the agency caring for the deceased. In the majority of circumstances, the personal effects are inventoried, stored, and, when the remains are released, the personal effects are turned over to those persons eligible to receive them, quite often family members. In those cases, no further actions are required other than to include detailed documentation of the action in the case file.
- In any incident, personal effects might be retained for forensic testing and can be considered evidence.

- In many jurisdictions, various laws and statutes codify the legal responsibility for the care and disposition of personal effects.
- In incidents that occur in remote areas that government agencies require some time to reach, and where local residents are nearby, looting of high-dollar items or "souvenir hunting" might, and often does, occur.
- In mass fatality incidents related to the carriage of passengers, such as on airlines, cruise ships, and railway trains, the search, recovery, care, and disposition of personal effects will be the responsibility of the carrier. Many carriers hire a third party to take control of the personal effects and oversee the disposition.

In these types of incidents associated, as well as unassociated, personal effects are recovered by law enforcement or private contractors. After release by law enforcement (if applicable) the personal effects are moved to a central location, and time is taken to determine the person is who is eligible to receive the effects. The option of cleaning, repairing, and restoring items is then offered to that person. Unclaimed personal effects are then often held for a long period of time before being destroyed. They are not auctioned off or used. In these cases, personal effects may also be held as evidence and subject to forensic testing prior to release by law enforcement.

Types of Personal Effects

For our purposes, the two types of personal effects are associated (Figure 7.2) and unassociated.

Figure 7.2 Typical associated personal effects. (Courtesy Kenyon International Emergency Services, Inc.)

Associated Personal Effects

Associated personal effects can be divided into three categories:

1. Items that are carried on a person and recovered on that person during the search and recovery
2. Items that are recovered from a mass fatality incident site that have distinct associating features such as a name on a passport in a purse or a name on medicine bottle in a suitcase (Figure 7.3)
3. Clothing articles recovered on remains

Note: Any items that are found on the remains should stay with them until they are removed at the mass fatality incident morgue.

Unassociated Personal Effects

Those items that are recovered from an incident site, but are not actually with remains, and have no name or other identifying information readily linking them to a specific deceased individual (Figure 7.4).

Note: You should expect to find many items with partial names on the item. However, if the name is not complete and does not exactly match that of a missing person, the item should be treated as unassociated.

How Personal Effects Are Recovered

Personal effects will be recovered in one of three ways.

1. **Recovered from remains:** Clothing items, jewelry, personal papers, and currency are the most common items recovered with remains. They are often associated by the fact that the personal effects were physically recovered from remains. When the remains are positively identified, the PE can then be associated with that positive identification. In some cases, however, the remains are never identified and the PE is then considered unassociated. Additionally, personal effects recovered from remains come under the control of government authorities at the same time the remains do. If the remains have not been disturbed, probably the personal effects have will not have been touched either.

2. **Recovered from the incident site by authorities:** Depending on the type of incident, many personal effects will be strewn about a site. Government responders (personnel working under a government flag)

Figure 7.3 Row of suitcases recovered from an aircraft accident. Note the varying conditions that are typical of such an accident. (Courtesy Kenyon International Emergency Services, Inc.)

Figure 7.4   In some cases, high-dollar items are recovered, although this is not necessarily typical of all incidents. (Courtesy Kenyon International Emergency Services, Inc.)

or private contractors are called in and assigned the job of recovering the PE. The amount, type, and condition of the PE recovered will depend on the incident, the terrain, the weather, and how fast control over the incident site was established.

3. **Recovered from the incident site by civilians:** In many instances, the general public may arrive at an incident site prior to the area's being brought under control. In these cases, some of the general public will pick up personal effects and turn them over to the first authorities they encounter. The problem with this is that the PE can be grouped or separated inappropriately.

Establishment of Personal Effects Operations

The scope of PE operations will depend on the scope of the incident. The first decision that must be made is who is responsible for the establishment, operation, and maintenance of PE operations. In most jurisdictions, the associated personal effects recovered on remains become the responsibility of the medical examiner.

As an essential part of preplanning, I strongly recommend that the responsibility of personal effects be assigned to a third party. By definition, a mass fatality incident is one that overwhelms the capabilities of the local resources. Therefore, during plan development or actual response, calling in private contractors with a proven track record of taking care of personal effects should be considered.

If a private contractor will not be hired, I recommend assigning responsibility for the search, recovery, care, and disposition of personal effects to a local major law enforcement agency. Although it is often the medical examiner who has responsibility for personal effects, many ME operations are not set up to handle large numbers of personal effects. On the other hand, most larger law enforcement agencies routinely handle large amounts of evidence (property), and are staffed and equipped to do so.

Once responsibility for the personal effects has been delegated, the next step is to begin the search and recovery operations.

Search Sequence

Before any area is searched, the following should occur.

- **Document the entire scene.** If the scene was not photographed thoroughly during the search and recovery of remains, it should be done at this time. The entire scene should be photographed using both still and video, color, and black-and-white film.
- **Establish perimeters.** Initial boundaries and perimeters should be established. Boundaries should be established several hundred yards beyond the end of the debris field. Large areas should be sectioned into quadrants. The overall boundaries and quadrants should be clearly marked.
- **Assess hazards.** After getting a look at the overall scene and talking with other incident mangers and specialists such as fire and HAZMAT personnel, the search leader should assess what the hazards are and what actions should be taken to mitigate them. Areas to consider include bloodborne pathogens, chemical contamination of the site, wreckage, and possibly animals such as snakes or other hazardous types that might inhabit the incident site (Figure 7.5).

After those actions are complete, each search team leader, who is responsible for the search team, assigning positions, and ensuring that all needed equipment is available and properly used, and that all procedures are followed. Each team leader must then assemble a team, which should include:

Figure 7.5 Responders searching the site of an aircraft accident for personal effects. Note the terrain and pieces of wreckage that definitely make this a hazardous site in which to work. (Courtesy Kenyon International Emergency Services, Inc.)

1. **Searchers**—responsible for locating the personal effects. They must be instructed not to separate "grouped" personal effects, nor to "group" separated personal effects. They will place the PE into bags.
2. **Search team photographers:** expected to photograph the recovery efforts and document as many of the recoveries as is practical.

Assemble Team

Personnel assigned to the team should gather. The team leaders should brief all team members on the following:

a. What to expect at the site
b. Each team member's specific job
c. The site hazards
d. What to expect

At this time, incident managers from other agencies should brief the search team as to items of interest to their particular organization. Although the primary function of this team is the finding of personal effects, searchers will often come upon useful investigatory objects such as a maintenance records, flight books, or obvious explosive-device components. The other agencies' incident managers should provide instruction for either marking the item or notifying the appropriate agency of the find.

A quick training session can also be conducted on the search pattern.

Draw equipment

Equipment should be collected from the logistics section or brought to the scene by the individual responders. (A detailed listing of equipment is provided in Appendix A.)

For the majority of recoveries, the basic equipment listed below is usually sufficient to accomplish the basic search-and-recovery functions. For very difficult recoveries, such as those from wreckage or very dangerous terrain, technical responders trained to use heavy and specialized tools should be brought in to complete the recovery.

Radios—The team leader and scribes should have two-way radios. The team leader should maintain communication with the incident manager and other team leaders. The scribes should have communication with each other and other search team scribes to ensure that duplicate numbers are not issued to items found.

Cameras—The preferred camera is a high-quality 35mm Single Lens Reflex (SLR),28-80 mm lens, and a mounted flash. Various speeds of film should be available to account for varying light conditions. Remember, these pictures may be used in criminal proceedings, in hearings to refute or support incident causation theories, or as a record on incident response.

Plastic bags of various sizes—Any of the commercially available food-storage bags will work just fine. These bags will be used to protect PE from further environmental or body fluid damage, to maintain group integrity and facilitate the recovery of a greater number of personal effects before a searcher has to return to the staging area.

Personal protective equipment and personal care items—Any required items to meet the OSHA standard and items for personal comfort such as hats, rain gear, insect repellent, and drinking water. Contaminated gloves should be removed and hands and face area sanitized before the consumption of water. Keeping hydrated is very important and requires frequent drinks, but it is not practical to have searchers leave the site. Therefore, they must take basic precautions before drinking the water. However, Searchers should not consume food or tobacco products on site and should stop for food or tobacco breaks.

(***Author's note:*** *While tobacco use is a contraindication to staying healthy and thereby reducing the effects of incident stress, many responders use tobacco and it is unrealistic to not address its use.*)

Enter the Site

The team, which has now been assembled and briefed, has drawn the required equipment and dressed in appropriate personal protective equipment, should now enter the site.

Site security should note exact time the teams enter the site.

Search and Recover

- Searchers form a line or assume whatever other search formation or pattern is appropriate.
- Searchers move out.
- Locate PE.
- Place PE into a plastic bag.
- Place bagged PE into a larger bag or other carrying device.
- Continue with the search.

Recovery Staging Area

Here the personal effects are staged for movement to the PE warehouse. The collected personal effects can be moved to the warehouse at any time. Movement should be accomplished with a law enforcement escort and the personal effects should be covered and moved in an appropriate vehicle such as semi-trailer or utility truck, never in any vehicle resembling a garbage or waste truck.

Depending on the site terrain and the number and condition of the deceased, the search can move along at a steady pace (Figure 7.5). The key is to be systematic, thorough, and have built-in system checks to catch mistakes before they impact the response.

Establishment of Personal Effects Warehouse

While few will argue that the PE must be recovered, many will argue about the degree to which they should be processed or what amount of disposition should be effected. I recommend that a PE warehouse be established to carry out complete processing and disposition of the personal effects.

The typical personal effects warehouse includes the following stations:

- Administration
- Receiving
- Storage
- Processing
- Disposition
- Destruction

Warehouse Considerations

Once the decision to establish a personal effects warehouse has been made, the next thing to discuss is where. Considerations for this are:

- Long-term availability of the facility. Disposition of personal effects is a lengthy process. In some recent cases, active PE operations continued well over two years after a major aviation accident. In most incidents, PE operations will almost always exceed all other operations except the incident investigation.
- Does the facility support compliance with all OSHA regulations? As we discussed in Chapter 4, personal effects may often be contaminated with various body fluids and other hazardous materials.
- Does it have controlled access, to keep the public—specifically photographers—back, but still allow access for vehicles and responders?
- Does the facility have the basics—water, sewer, electrical power, ventilation, and climate control?
- Is the facility single story and does it have an access door that can accommodate material-handling equipment such as pallet jacks and small forklifts? If a multistory building is chosen, it should have a heavy-duty lift or elevator.

The decision on where to establish a personal effects facility need not be made immediately, unlike the decision on what facility to use for the establishment of the mass fatality incident morgue. The immediate focus will be on the establishment of the morgue and the recovery operations, so the person assigned the responsibility for establishing the PE operations will have some time. However, to accommodate those personal effects that might be recovered from the incident site or brought to the authorities by civilians, an initial PE staging area should be established.

Administration

The administration station serves as the brain and nerve center of the PE warehouse. Its primary functions are to:

1. **Collect and collate all lists of persons eligible to receive effects (PEREs)**

The personal effects warehouse administration section will collect the information gathered at the family assistance center or directly provided by families, survivors of the incident, family attorneys, or legal representatives. They will begin to sort the information. At this time, the information gathered should be:

- Name of the victim or survivor
- Medical Examiner's victim case number
- Person eligible to receive effects or their designated representatives

This information should be placed into individual files organized by the victim's or survivor's last name.

In some cases, family members or survivors will attempt to offer descriptions of their own or loved one's personal effects. That information is often not very useful. For associated effects, the items are already linked to a particular person. For unassociated personal effects there are often simply too many items to go through and try to identify based on descriptions.

2. Manage or administer case files

As the personal effects are taken through the PE warehouse process, additional documents are created. When these records are not being used they should be kept at the PE warehouse administration station. Any time the records are removed they should be signed for and a sign-out card placed in the file.

At the conclusion of the incident recovery, the case files should be filed in accordance with local laws and customs for incident records.

3. Act as the single point of contact (POC) for all personal effects operations

Any request for information should be passed to and answered by the administration station to avoid answering questions twice or not asking the right person. Media inquiries should always be handled by trained media spokespersons. However, inquiries from family members or other response agencies should be directed here. As organized, the administration station should always have the most current and complete information.

The administration station also serves to coordinate work shifts and to procure and maintain equipment and supplies.

4. Monitor status board

A simple status board should be established at the onset of an incident and maintained throughout. In large incidents, a computerized status board should be used. Status boards are very simple, sometimes created with spreadsheets, but more often drawn on large bristol board and tacked to large open walls. A sample status board is shown in Figure 7.6.

The administration station should update the status board any time a change is made to the number, condition, or identification of personal effects.

Personal Effects Status Board

Incident: _____ .   Page: _____ of _____

Primary PE Agency: _____

Current Case #	Previous Case #	Date Recovered	Item Recovered	Associated Name		Disposition	
				Last	First	Received	Completed

NO ENTRY ON THIS DOCUMENT WILL BE ERASED. ALL ERRONEOUS ENTRIES WILL BE LINED THRU
AND INITIALED BY THE PERSON MAKING THE CORRECTION

Figure 7.6 Suggested layout for a personal effects operations status board.

Initial Receiving Operations

The initial actions taken with associated and unassociated personal effects are the same, however, after some basic procedures, the process becomes very different. In this section I will first discuss the basic procedures, and will then go over the receiving and processing of associated and unassociated personal effects separately (Figure 7.7).

Figure 7.7 Specialist inventorying and examining various personal effects. (Courtesy Kenyon International Emergency Services, Inc.)

The receiving section should also maintain the secure storage area. Key points to remember about the storage area:

- The area should have only one entrance.
- Shelving material should be strong enough to safely support the weight of an undetermined number of personal effects.
- All persons entering the secure storage area should be logged in and out of the area on a log that should include:
    a.Name of person entering
    b.Agency of person entering
    c.The case numbers of any items being carried in or out of the secure area
    d.The purpose of the entry into the secure area

(Note: If the secure area is not manned continuously, it should have an alarm or monitoring system installed.)
- All recovered personal effects should come to the receiving station. Here they should first be checked, if not done previously, to determine if:

    - This is a piece of evidence or item relevant to the mass fatality incident investigation. Items such as aircraft maintenance forms or an item such as an explosive component from a bomb might be inadvertently picked up and turned in as personal effects.

- If the PE contains fragments of human remains

Personal effects that are received as part of an intact group, such as those recovered in a single logical item such as purse, wallet, or suitcase should remain an intact group. Similarly, several personal effects recovered from one body should be treated as an intact group. These personal effects are almost always defined as "group."

On the other hand, personal effects that were recovered separately but placed into a box or large bag for ease of transportation should be treated as separate, or "individual," personal effects.

The person receiving the item at this station should first determine if they have been given an associated or unassociated item.

A challenge you undoubtedly will face is having personal effects marked with clearly identifiable names of people who were not involved in the incident. For example, when a person goes on a flight, borrows a suitcase from a friend, then is killed when the plane crashes. The person traveling is most likely properly listed on the manifest, but the name on the suitcase is the owner's, not the borrower's.

If the personal effects display a name, and that name is also the name of a known victim or survivor, the personal effects should be considered associated.

If the personal effects display a name and that name is *not* the name of a known victim or survivor, then I suggest that the items be treated as unassociated.

At this point, the operation flows should follow different procedures for processing and disposition of associated and unassociated personal effects.

Associated Personal Effects Receiving

Once the determination is made that the personal effects being received can be classified as associated, the following actions will be done:

1. Conduct a joint inventory.

Conduct an inventory that involves both the person receiving the PE and the person turning the effects over. Every item should be inventoried and both parties should sign the inventory. In some cases, individuals turning personal effects over to the warehouse will not want to participate in or sign a joint inventory, nonetheless, the agency operating the PE warehouse should still immediately inventory the items and establish accountability. Any refusal to participate and sign the joint inventory should be noted on the inventory form.

When conducting the inventory, separate sheets should be used for each, or each group of, personal effects that will be assigned a unique case number.

As each item is accepted, a narrative description of it should be placed on an inventory form that should reflect generic terms such as:

- "Yellow-colored metal" for items believed to be made of gold
- "Silver-colored metal" for items believed to be made from silver or platinum
- "Clear stone-like" for items believed to be diamonds
- "Colored stone-like" for items believed to be other precious gems
- Watch, with name "Rolex," as opposed to Rolex watch

Although writing inventories in such a manner is time consuming, it is the best way to protect your agency and yourself against possible false claims. Unfortunately, some people will take advantage of the mass fatality incident to achieve monetary gain.

Inventory forms should also have multiple signature and date blocks. Any time personal effects are being processed, the individual doing the processing should sign the chain of custody acknowledging that all the listed items are present at that time. If a discrepancy is discovered, they should immediately notify a supervisor, who should investigate and determine what has occurred. Further, if the personal effects are turned over to a different agency or to the PERE, a joint inventory should be conducted on the outgoing items and the inventory form signed.

2. Remove dangerous goods.

If, during the inventory, dangerous items such as flammables or items containing liquids that could break and damage other items should be removed and stored separately or destroyed. Prior to destroying any items, you should check with your legal counsel to ensure that it can be destroyed. Later in this chapter I recommend some procedures to follow for the destruction of personal effects.

3. Assign a case number.

If not already done as part of the recovery operation, a case number should be assigned to the personal effects.

There are several options available for this. It really does not matter what system is used, as long as it meets a few basic requirements. Those requirements are:

- It should be simple.
- It should easy to enter into a computer database to be tracked at any time.
- It should not allow for duplication of numbers.
- It should not be changed once established.

The chosen system should make allowance for personal effects recovered as part of an intact group or associated to one group to be given an overall number as well as providing individual numbers for the individual PE of that group. For example, a purse containing 25 individual items is recovered and assigned a case number of 100. Each item in the purse would then be assigned a number such as 100-1 through 100-25. Again, it does not matter what system you use as long as a unique number is assigned to each PE recovered.

Note: I do not recommend creating separate systems to track associated and unassociated personal effects. Quite often personal effects initially considered associated could later become unassociated and vice versa.

A durable tag containing the assigned case number should then be affixed to the personal effect. This can be done in several ways, such as using plastic lock snap ties, "tagger" guns (those used by department stores to attach retail price tags to articles of clothing), or paper tags with twine.

In the case of items to which tags cannot be attached, a tag should be marked and placed into a clear plastic bag or paper bag along with the PE. The case number should also be written on the bag.

At this station, personal effects that are received either as individual items or grouped should be placed into a single bag for which just one case number tag is prepared. At the processing station, further case number tags and separate bagging of items will take place. The goal of the receiving station is to simply get control and accountability of the personal effects.

4. Initiate a case file folder.

The case file is contained in a simple folder that should be large enough to hold any documentation that will be created at the morgue. At a minimum, the case file folder should have:

- The name associated with the PE neatly printed on the outside.
- The case number printed legibly on the outside.
- A printed checklist that includes each station. As stations are completed, notes can be made on the checklist. When the case file folder is reviewed for quality control it is easy to verify that all stations have been completed.
- A log showing dates, start, and completion times for any actions involving the personal effects.

The case file folder is then placed in a file stand or similar holder where it is easy to retrieve when the processing of the personal effects begins.

5. Place personal effects into storage bags.

If the personal effects are wet or damp, they should be laid out to dry and consideration should be given to having available large butane heaters or other commercial-type drying devices. Dry items should be placed into storage bags. Durable items such as metals, or other items that have little contamination and are not likely to be at all damp can also be placed into plastic bags.

Large bulky or items that may give off gases should be placed into paper bags that will allow the gases and moisture to dissipate.

The bags and case file should then be placed into the controlled storage area.

6. Update status board.

The status board maintained by the administration station should be updated to reflect the arrival of each item or group of items to the warehouse.

Associated Personal Effects Processing

The processing station is the second station to which the personal effects are brought.

The role of the processing station in a PE operation is fairly straightforward. However, do not mistake straightforward for easy. As mentioned earlier, working with personal effects can be emotionally difficult. Additionally, the necessary "inventory" controls and ability to document all actions is quite important.

Associated personal effects, since they have been directly related to a victim or survivor, should be processed first. They are also most likely the most important personal effects.

The processing station's primary functions and flow are to collect the personal effects from the storage area. Processors should go to the PE storage area and collect a case file and corresponding bag of personal effects (see Figure 7.8). They should then take both to the processing work area, which might be only a table in a well-lit and ventilated area.

Once in the work area they should do the following:

- Remove the personal effects from the bags.
- Check the inventory against the actual items; if any are missing the processor immediately notifies a supervisor, who should complete an

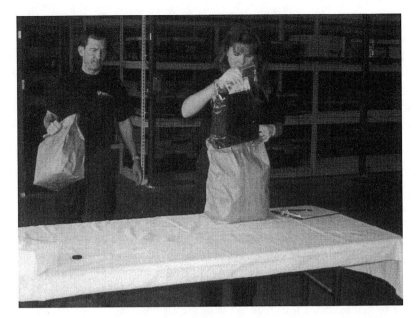

Figure 7.8 Two responders remove personal effects from a secure storage area to a clean work area. Note the plastic bag containing a PE and its identifying tag. (Courtesy Kenyon International Emergency Services, Inc.)

investigation into the discrepancy. If all the personal effects are present the processor signs the chain of custody form.

- Items that have been contaminated should be decontaminated. If this is impossible, they should be segregated and marked for destruction. This is then noted in the case file log and inventory sheet.
- Items that are damaged and very dirty should have a notation made on the inventory form. Remember, the PERE is often a family member who will see the inventory form, therefore the terms and descriptions used should be carefully considered. I recommend not using terms such as "burned" or "shredded," I would say "damaged" or "almost completely destroyed." Although it might not seem like a big distinction it often makes a big difference to the families.
- Individual case number tags are made for each personal effect.
- The case number tag are attached to the personal effect.
- A photograph of the personal effect, with the case number attached to it or resting next to it is taken.
- The personal effect is neatly placed into a storage bag.
- If the personal effect is part of an "associated group" the individual bags should be placed into a large single bag or container.
- The personal effects are returned to the controlled storage area.

The case file should then be updated and returned to the administration station.

All associated personal effects are processed prior to moving on to disposition. This is for several reasons. To begin with, there will probably be several different bags of personal effects associated with one victim or survivor, but they will most likely not be received all at once. Also, initial notifications of the associated effects should be mailed to all PERE at about the same time to avoid any perceptions of preferential treatment to certain victims.

Associated Personal Effects Disposition

Once all the associated personal effects have been processed, disposition can begin. Disposition is contacting the PERE to determine their desires and then carrying those desires out within the limits of your resources and the applicable laws.

The dynamics of the incident will also drive some of the choices to be made. For example, in some cases, laws may require that the PERE be given the choice of having damaged items repaired or cleaned (such as in aviation accidents.) In other cases, there may be no mechanism in place to pay for cleaning or repair of personal effects and the PERE must take them as is. If possible, it is always better to give the PERE the choice.

After all associated personal effects have been processed and correlated to victims or survivors, certified letters should be sent to each PERE. The letters should briefly explain the circumstances of the recovery, that some of the personal effects may have been contaminated and could not be decontaminated and were therefore destroyed (if applicable), explain the process for completing the enclosed forms, and also explain the process for the unassociated personal effects.

Unassociated Personal Effects Receiving

Once the determination is made that the personal effects are unassociated, the following actions should occur:

1. Issue a receipt or sign for the item.

In some cases, individuals turning PE over to the warehouse will want a signed document to show that they have done so. A simple receipt should be prepared and signed.

Narrative descriptions of the item, using generic terms such as those suggested in the earlier inventory, should be placed on the receipt form.

2. Remove dangerous goods.

If, during the inventory, dangerous items such as flammables or liquids in containers that could break and damage other items are received, they should be removed and stored separately or destroyed. Prior to destroying any items, you should check with your legal counsel to ensure that the item may be destroyed. Later in this chapter I recommend some procedures to follow for the destruction of PE.

3. Assign a case number.

If not already done as part of the recovery operation, a case number, using a system such as described earlier, should be assigned to the personal effects, and the items should then be tagged or placed into a clear plastic bag and labeled.

A durable tag, with the assigned case number written onto the tag should then be affixed to the personal effect. This can be done in several ways. Some suggested ways are the use of plastic lock-snap ties, "tagger" guns (those used by department stores to attach retail price tags), or paper tags with twine.

In the case of items to which tags cannot be attached, a tag or label should be written out and placed into a clear bag or paper bag with the personal effect. The case number should further be written onto the bag.

At this station personal effects that are received or associated as a group should be placed into one bag. Only one case number tag is prepared. At the processing station, further case number tags and separate bagging of items will occur. The goal of the receiving station is to simply get control and accountability of the personal effects.

4. Enter the case number onto a database form or into a database.

Once a case number has been assigned, it should be entered on a database form or directly into a database. You can use any of several different databases. I recommend using whatever is the simplest system for your agency. Minimum recommended information fields are:

- Case number field
- Personal effect description field
- Disposition field

Unassociated Personal Effects Processing

Processors should go to the personal effects storage area and collect a container of unassociated personal effects, which should then be taken to the processing work area. This can be just a table in a well-lit and ventilated area.

Once in the work area they should then do the following:

- Remove the personal effects from the bags.
- Verify the case number against the existing database.
- Thoroughly check the PE to ensure that any associating information has not been overlooked. If associating information is discovered, the item should be treated as associated and processed as such.
- Items that have been contaminated should be decontaminated. If they cannot be decontaminated they should be segregated and marked for destruction. This information should be noted on the database form.
- Items that are damaged and very dirty should have a notation made on database form. Remember, the PERE is often a family member and so will see the database form, therefore the terms and descriptions used should be carefully considered. I recommend not using terms such as "burned" or "shredded," I would say "damaged" or "almost completely destroyed." Although it might not seem like a big distinction it often makes a big difference to the families.
- Individual case number tags should then be made for each PE.
- The case number tag should then be attached to the PE.
- A photograph of the PE, with the case number attached to it or resting next to it, should be taken.
- The PE should then be neatly placed into a storage bag.
- The case number should then be written onto the case file number.

If the PE is part of a "group," the individual bags should be placed into a single large bag or container.

- The personal effects should then be returned to the controlled storage area.
- The case file should be updated and returned to the administration station.

Unassociated Personal Effects Disposition

Once all unassociated personal effects have been processed, disposition can begin.

For unassociated PE, disposition involves:

- Contacting the PEREs to determine if they desire to participate in the unassociated personal effects process

- Providing all PERE who wish to participate the availability to view all unassociated personal effects and make claims for the effects
- Resolving multiple claims for the same items

The dynamics of the incident will also drive the answers to some of these questions. For example, in some cases laws may require that the PERE be given the choice of having damaged items repaired or cleaned (such as in aviation accidents.) In other cases, there may be no mechanism to pay for cleaning or repair of personal effects and the PERE must take them as is. If possible, it is always better to give the PERE the choice.

To do this, the first thing you must do is determine how you will provide the PERE the opportunity to view the personal effects. In some cases, pictorial catalogues of all the unassociated effects have been produced and sent to the families, in others the unassociated PE were laid out in a large warehouse and the PERE were allowed to walk through and claim items.

Just as the incident dynamics play a key role in deciding what actions you can take for the cleaning and repair of personal effects, so do they act in deciding how the unassociated effects are made available for return. The processing and distribution of unassociated personal effects is very costly. In transportation incidents, the carrier's insurance companies will pay for these actions, in natural disasters or non-insured incidents, the funds may not be available to pay for such actions.

If a pictorial catalogue or layout is going to be the method of distribution, the database and pictures must be organized in a clear fashion to make it easy for the PERE to go through and pick out the personal effects they want to claim.

After the decision has been made as to what method will be used to effect disposition, certified letters should be sent to all PERE who have stated willingness to participate in the unassociated PE process. The letters should briefly explain the following:

- The disposition procedures (catalogue or layout)
- The circumstances of the recovery
- That some of the personal effects may have been contaminated and could not be decontaminated and so were destroyed (if applicable)
- The process for completing the enclosed forms
- The process for multiple claims
- How long unclaimed personal effects will be kept

  • How unclaimed personal effects will be disposed of after the spec-
    ified holding period

Effecting Unassociated Disposition

Once you have received the disposition instructions back from the PERE,
simply carry them out.

  If you receive multiple claims for a single item, consult with your legal
counsel to determine the best method for resolving them. In many cases,
once PEREs learn of a multiple claim, several claims will be dropped. This
is not say that PEREs claim personal effects that they are not entitled to, but
quite the opposite; they are so concerned about other families that they will
give up an item just to make it easier for someone else. In the same light,
unassociated currency and other negotiable instruments are often never
claimed.

  If personal effects are mailed, insured mail with return receipt requested
should be used, or if the PERE receives PE in person, a joint inventory form
should be signed.

  Certain key points to remember:

  • Carefully package the PE for shipment; further damage is inexcusable.
  • Package the PE in the manner in which you would want to receive
    them; remember, in many cases, they are the only tangible reminders
    of a lost life.
  • Ensure that delivery will be made when someone is available to receive
    it. You do not want the item to be left at the door.
  • Be sensitive to the timing of correspondence and delivery of personal
    effects. Watch for holidays, anniversary of the loss dates, and if possi-
    ble, for anniversaries or birthdays of the deceased.

Destruction of Personal Effects

Once the PEREs or survivors have all had an opportunity to claim both
associated and unassociated personal effects, and any predetermined storage
periods have elapsed, those personal effects scheduled for destruction should
be destroyed. Although there are several possible methods, I recommend that
the PE be incinerated to the point that no recognizable forms are left. This
type of incineration can easily be accomplished at local waste facilities, hospitals, or heavy-metal-manufacturing plants.

  When a PERE gives notification that a PE is to be destroyed, it should
be marked with a special tag indicating that it is scheduled for destruction.
The PE database should be updated with the information.

When it is time for the destruction, a two-person team should:

- Gather all documents authorizing destruction
- Collect all personal effects tagged for destruction
- Compare the gathered documentation, which includes case numbers, with the case number tags attached to the personal effects
- Prepare certificates of destruction for each personal effect
- Destroy the personal effects
- Take before, during, and after video or photographs of the destruction

The original certificate of destruction (Figure 7.9) should then be placed into the case file and a copy sent to the PERE.

Long-Term Storage of Personal Effects

Remember that the PE operations may take several years to resolve. In incidents where a third party or private company is not responsible for the payment of operational costs, strict deadlines may be established for the PERE to claim the personal effects. On the other hand, in cases involving private corporations, some laws currently mandate the retention of unclaimed personal effects for a minimum of 18 months, therefore provisions should be made to provide secure storage of the unclaimed items.

Again I recommend that strong consideration be given to using well-established and experienced private contractors. Nonetheless, if a jurisdiction or private corporation insists on dealing with the PE issue in-house, I recommend that they take the following steps:

- Locate a secure facility in which to store the PE (Figure 7.10).
- Keep the PE in the original marked bags.
- Conduct a monthly inventory of the bags by case number.
- Maintain access logs showing the inventories and documenting any disturbance or removal of PE

PE Operations Resources

The business of personal effects operations is resource intensive and requires very special people with a wide range of skills. I recommend you consider the following resources when establishing, operating, and maintaining your PE operations.

- Military mortuary affairs specialist
- Funeral directors

CERTIFICATE OF PERSONAL EFFECTS DESTRUCTION

Case # _____   Recovery Date: _____   Page _____ of _____

Property Owner *(If known)*: _____   Location of Destruction: _____

Date Destruction Ordered: _____   *(Street Address)*

Method of Destruction: _____   *(City, State, ZIP Code)*

CASE #	INVENTORY DESCRIPTION	QUANTITY	REASON FOR DESTRUCTION

Destruction Approved By: _____   Destruction Completed By: _____   Destruction Witnessed By: _____

(Printed Name & Title)   *(Printed Name & Title)*   *(Printed Name & Title)*

(Signature)   *(Signature)*   *(Signature)*

NO ENTRY ON THIS DOCUMENT WILL BE ERASED. ALL ERRONEOUS ENTRIES WILL BE LINED THRU AND INITIALED BY THE PERSON MAKING THE CORRECTION

Figure 7.9 Suggested PE certificate of destruction.

- Interpreters
- Law enforcement evidence bureau personnel
- Data entry personnel
- Military supply personnel
- Local, state, or federal inventory control specialists
- Notary publics
- Legal counsel
- Photographers
- Jewelers
- Janitorial or maintenance staff

Figure 7.10 An alarmed, secure PE storage area. Note shelving and various storage containers. (Courtesy Kenyon International Emergency Services, Inc.)

A pathologist and a criminal or technical specialist relative to the type of incident should be available on an on-call basis to assist in the receiving section during the initial screening of the personal effects. Additionally, although probably not needed on a full-time basis, a qualified critical incident stress debriefer or crisis counselor should be available for the operational staff and should make periodic visits, walking through the PE warehouse to personally visit and check on the responders.

Just as in the mass fatality incident morgue, PE operations are no place for people who do not wish to work there, knew any of the victims, are under the age of 18, or lack maturity. The risks are just too great.

Summary

Next to the mass fatality incident morgue operations, no other aspect of the overall operation will probably be as challenging as the recovery, processing, and disposition of the personal effects. It takes very special people who can effectively communicate with the families, follow their wishes, and at the same time follow the law.

Proper recovery, processing, and disposition will take time, require manpower, and cost a significant amount of money. However, it is something that must be done, and done well, even if not required by law.

Family Assistance

8

No matter the cause of the incident or the size of the response force, the success of any incident response will depend on how well the families were cared for. As I mentioned at the beginning of this book, there is no magic pill that will satisfy everyone, you are, after all, dealing with the death of someone who was very dear to someone else. There is, however, one thing you can do to ensure that *no one* will be satisfied—handle family assistance badly.

Family Needs

Most families want very little, in fact, no more than anyone really has the right to expect, and that is:

- They want information as soon as it becomes available, and they would like it before the media is told about it.
- They want their loved ones cared for in a dignified and respectful manner.
- They want somebody to listen to them when they have concerns or just want to talk about their loss.
- When they are at the incident location they want their physical needs taken care of.

In short, they should be treated with compassion, given candid answers to their questions, and provided with the basic care that is routinely afforded to families when they lose someone they love. The challenge to the mass fatality incident manager and responder is to remember those needs and provide for them.

Now more then ever, families do not wait by the phone for news, but actually travel to mass fatality incident sites. They often arrive within the first 24 hours of an incident and stay until the recovery of remains is complete or near completion. Additionally, not just one, but often several members of the victims' extended families come to the incident site.

In addition to those who travel to the site, many other family members and friends will flood the jurisdiction where the incident occurred with thousands of phone calls inquiring about the status of their loved ones and friends. In many cases they are just trying to determine if their loved ones were actually involved in the incident.

To make matters worse in natural disasters, the local phone companies will usually automatically shut down all incoming calls so that lines remain clear for responders and official calls. On the other hand, in commercial incidents such as transportation accidents or building collapses, the news media will start full coverage almost instantly, broadcasting agencies involved and telephone numbers for people to call. Unfortunately, even people who really do not have a valid need or realistic concern will call those numbers immediately.

To address these concerns, some laws have recently been passed mandating sufficient toll-free phone numbers to enable people to inquire about an incident. The problem with this is that no one has ever really researched just how many calls are actually received, how long each call lasts, and how many of the calls are actually from family members. Additionally, people calling into the toll-free lines expect to be given information, when really the call is for the agency or government to gather information. The information the callers are given is usually the same as what is available from the media, in other words, "Flight XX crashed into Anytown at 8:00 PM tonight. We are still checking the local hospitals to determine the number of survivors, etc." The callers, on the other hand, want to inquire specifically about one person's status, when that information is just not rapidly available.

The best way to resolve these issues and meet the needs of the families and friends is have your media people immediately put out the information they know, and tell why that is all they know. Then quickly establish a family assistance center.

Note that I use the terms family, relatives, and friends. That is because some people simply do not have family, or are so distant from their families that they would never have reason to suspect their relative was a potential victim of a mass fatality incident. However, most people have close friends who were aware of their travel plans and locations. Remember, all of these relatives and friends will play a key role in your being able to get the ante-mortem records used for identification.

Family Assistance Inquiry Center

This part of your operation should last no more than 24 to 48 hours. Its functions are to (1) provide basic information, (2) screen calls to determine which callers really have relatives or friends missing and presumed to be victims of the incident, (3) gather information about those missing persons, and (4) gather return-call information for further contact.

1. **Provide Basic Information**
   - Tell the caller what is known about the incident—only what is known, not what you think.
   - Tell them that they are going to be asked some basic questions, and establish that they are the appropriate person for you to deal with. Inform them that as soon as possible a person will call them back with more information and also perhaps more instructions, if appropriate.
   - Give an accurate estimate of how long it will take for the caller to be called back.
   - Inquire the age of the caller, and if they are alone. If the caller is a minor and alone or someone who is obviously distressed, the inquiry center should attempt to have a qualified professional near the caller's location go to the caller and provide assistance if needed. Communities should establish such points of contact through national service organizations and religious groups in prior to incidents so they can be called upon if disaster strikes.

2. **Screen Calls**
   - Ask why they think the person(s) the caller is asking about is involved in the mass fatality incident.
   - What is their relation to the person(s)?
   - If they are not family, do they know the family and do they have contact information?

3. **Information about the Missing**
   - When was the person(s) last seen?
   - What was each person(s) full name, age, and, if possible, date of birth?

4. **Gather Return Call Information**
   - The phone operator should ask the caller what number they can be reached at, what is the best time to call, and who they should speak with.
   - If callers plan to come to the incident site, they should also be asked for the name and number of family dentists. They should also be

told that if they are in possession of any dental or other medical records they should bring them with them.

Your company or jurisdiction should have plans established for the immediate establishment of a call center. Today many agencies have hired third party contractors to maintain call centers just to respond to questions about mass fatality incidents; others have joined with similar businesses to form mutual aid agreements that will assist the one agency in its time of crisis. Whatever system you use, it should have:

- Professionally trained operators who will not take personally any abuse that might be given to them, but will understand it is the emotion of the incident
- The capability of handling several hundred calls simultaneously without cutting callers off
- Multiple language capabilities
- Automated systems that can collate the information collected
- The ability to deal with different types of people

Note: Both private businesses and agencies that are potentially involved daily in mass fatality incidents would be well advised to institute a phone-home program for their employees. This is nothing more than a plan that states whenever your agency is involved in a mass fatality incident all of your employees who might have been part of the incident (such as workers at a refinery that has an explosion or train crews when a train in the company has an accident) simply call home as soon as possible and let their families know that they are all right. Their families would then start calling any other individuals who might call an inquiry center. Although this will not eliminate the number of actual non-victim-related calls to the inquiry center, it should cut down on some of them.

Family Assistance Without Establishing a Center

Even if you do not establish a Joint Family Assistance Center, information such as antemortem identification records and disposition instructions must be collected from the families and official notification of positive identification must be made.

The best way to do that is through a Joint Family Assistance Center, but if you are not establishing one, some system of collecting and disseminating the required information must be developed.

Another point for consideration is that even if you do establish a center not all families will travel to it. Some provision must be made for contacting those families. The best way to do that is through reciprocal agreements between medical examiners or law enforcement agencies.

One of the center's main purposes is to gather contact information to call back family members or friends. In some incidents, specifically those involving private industry, an industry representative will initially return calls confirming that the families' loved one was on board a particular aircraft or in a particular section of an industrial plant when it exploded. This should not be confused with an official notification of positive identification. Although in many cases the victim is actually dead, that is not always the case. Official notification should come only after the establishment of positive identification.

In those cases when industry is not required to make such a notification, the next call should come from the personnel collecting the antemortem information.

Three basic segments of information must be exchanged, either at the family assistance center or through other means.

1. Antemorten Records Collection

Trained death investigators or funeral directors should meet with or contact each family and attempt to get as much information as they can about the victims. Many agencies have developed very detailed questionnaires, the purpose of which is simply to collect information that will help the medical examiner gather all the antemortem records necessary for him to compare to the postmortem records that will be created at the mass fatality incident morgue. It is during these interviews that a determination will be made if law enforcement or death investigation agencies local to the home of the victim(s) should be contacted to go to the home and collect fingerprints and DNA donor samples from personal hygiene items.

Some family members may even bring antemortem records with them to the family assistance center or may have instructed their family medical caregivers to forward the records to the family assistance center. The person collecting the information should then pass the information sheets and recommendations on collecting fingerprints or DNA to the morgue administration section, where the information is collated and any additional information is collected.

2. Official Notification—Positive Identification

Once positive identification of victims has been established, the medical examiner or a representative of the ME's office should personally notify the families. Although they will most likely have accepted that their relatives are dead, they may still have some hope that they were not involved in the incident. The official notification will finally bring home the fact that their loved ones were victims of the mass fatality incident and have, in fact, been killed.

During this notification a trained grief counselor and, if desired, an appropriate religious advisor should be present.

3. Disposition Instructions

After families have been officially notified of the positive identification, they should be asked about after care instructions. This is also an appropriate time for the medical examiner, in consultation with legal counsel, to determine who is the proper person authorized to direct disposition (PADD) of the remains. The PADD varies from one jurisdiction to another. Once the PADD has been determined, their wishes should be determined and, if practical and allowed by law, carried out.

The medical examiner must also decide if the PADD will be informed that multiple releases of the remains may occur. The medical examiner needs to know if the PADD wants to wait until all recovery efforts are complete and then receive all fragments of remains at once. Or perhaps they want to receive those fragments that the medical examiner currently has positively identified, and then have the medical examiner effect disposition of any other fragments later recovered or identified.

Family Escort

Another important part of taking care of the families is the assignment of family escorts or family representatives. The system works well within the center, but it can also work well if a center is not established and for those families that do not travel to the incident site.

Family escorts are often volunteers from an industry involved in the incident, or local people who volunteer to help. One role of the family escort is to look after the physical needs of the families, ensuring they have shelter, food, and transportation. Many families will not need these things, but they should be offered them and they should make the decision to accept or decline what they want. Another role of the family escort is to link up the family members with the appropriate person or agency to answer any questions they may have. The family escort is there to listen and offer support.

Family escorts should have crisis training to include:

- An overall understanding of the roles and responsibilities of various agencies in a mass fatality incident so that they can better explain the flow of events to the families
- An understanding of what assistance programs are available to the families, such as crime victims' compensation, and grief counseling services such as those offered through the Red Cross/Red Crescent.
- An understanding of the laws regarding the collection of and use of antemortem medical records for identification. (In previous incidents, families have reported that antemortem medical records given to industry family escorts or representatives for delivery to the ME were copied by the industry representative and later used in court to help lower the payment of damages.)
- Communication training on how to talk and deal with people who have just suffered a loss.

Family escorts with a variety of language skills should also be available, and, if appropriate, signing interpreters for the hearing impaired.

The Joint Family Assistance Center

The word "joint" is added because many organizations will play a key role in the establishment, operation, and maintenance of the center. The lead agency to establish the joint family assistance center should be an agency like the Red Cross/Red Crescent or a local victims' assistance coordinator. The mission of the joint family assistance center is to provide a secure location where families or friends can:

- Gather to wait for more information
- Be interviewed to collect antemortem information
- Receive information briefings from the ME, investigative agencies, industry involved with the incident, and government representatives prior to such information being released to the media
- Be told about the positive identification of their relatives, and hence given the official notification of death
- Make disposition arrangements for the deceased
- Meet with grief counselors
- Escape the media blitz

In short, the center is a sanctuary for many people who are experiencing the same fears and feelings.

Establishment of a Joint Family Assistance Center

While the medical examiner is being called to the scene of the mass fatality incident, the lead agency in establishing the center should be finding a suitable location and beginning to establish the center.

Some key points to consider, no matter where you establish a center:

- Be sensitive to the cultural differences among the families.
- Limit the number of uniformed personnel present at the center. Depending on the particular incident, you might have a large number of undocumented aliens or others who fear uniformed authority. Remember the goal is to resolve the incident, not to enforce unrelated laws.
- Have some plain-clothes law enforcement personnel in the area, as in some cases, families do get physical with the responders.
- Have access to translators.

Joint Family Assistance Center Considerations

Once the decision to establish a center has been made, the next thing to think about is where. Considerations for this are:

- Immediate availability of the facility—In some cases, such as local incidents, families will start to arrive immediately; in other cases, they will start to arrive in numbers within 24 hours.
- Long term availability of the facility—For planning purposes, expect the center to operate for up to 30 days after the incident.
- Controlled access—Is it possible to keep the public, and specifically photographers, back, but still allow access for family members?
- Availability of the basics—Are water, sewer, electrical power, ventilation, and climate control readily accessed? Can the telephone and data transmission capabilities be rapidly expanded?
- Proximity—Is the facility close enough to the incident site so the ME and other responders can travel relatively easily between the site and the center to conduct briefings, yet far enough away so family members need not view the site if they do not want to?
- Modifications for those with disabilities—Can people with physical handicaps easily access the facility and use the amenities provided?
- Dining facilities—Are there restaurants nearby?

The decision on where to establish a family assistance center must be made rapidly. A hotel or motel is often a good choice. Most of today's larger and even many of the smaller hotels or motels have small-business centers with the capability to greatly expand phone centers and data transmission lines. Almost any hotel will have multiple private rooms that can be used for a variety of purposes, and most are near restaurants.

Naturally, the hotel or motel will have to relocate other guests and will certainly charge for their services. I have never seen or heard of any business unwilling to provide support during a mass fatality incident, in fact, quite the opposite—most offer help before it is requested.

If the mass fatality incident occurs in an area where the majority of the victims are local, sleeping rooms won't be necessary, but I suggest you still consider a hotel or motel for its other favorable aspects.

Joint Family Assistance Center Layout

The Joint Family Assistance Center should be organized to accommodate the following operational sections:

- Reception station
- Administration station
- Large lounge or break room
- Supervised children's area
- Multiple small briefing or counseling rooms
- Large briefing room
- Business and communications center
- Medical-aid room
- Small chapel area

Reception Station

The reception station plays many key roles. It is responsible for:

- **Controlling access to the center**—This can be a difficult process, as you may not yet know victims' names. If you already have a manifest or list of the missing from the inquiry center, you should use that list. If not, you should screen people in much the same manner as the inquiry center does. You should always check a photo identification and even consider issuing your own special ID badge for family members so that it is easier for them to come and go from the center.

In all but the largest mass fatality incidents, within the first 24 hours you should have an accurate manifest or list of missing persons to go by. You should then reconfirm the people who have checked into the center to verify that they in fact belong there.

- **Welcoming the family members or friends to the center and assigning a family escort**—Not a difficult job, but very important; after the family members have been allowed access they should be greeted and, if resources allow, assigned a family escort, whose job is to serve as that family's single point of contact for all questions and concerns. Escorts should be assigned to no more than one family.

Administration Station

The administration station plays many key roles, which are:

- **Maintaining the database**—A simple database of who has come to the center and any of their contact information should be collected and maintained. This database should be merged with that of the inquiry call center after it is closed down. In that way, contacting family members who are not present should be easier.
- **Maintaining assistance files**—Any assistance provided to the family members should be noted and copies of all receipts and actions taken should be filed. The files should be set up based on the victims' last names. All information for any person who is a family member of that victim should go into that file. When it is time to account for the money spent, these files will be necessary to establish a proper audit trail.
- **Coordinating security**—All security issues and concerns should be managed by this section's personnel. They should coordinate shift changes and ensure that the proper authorities are notified whenever there are any problems.

Plenty of plainclothes law enforcement should be present in the area to ensure that only authorized family members gain access to the center, and to apprehend those individuals who attempt to gain entrance by false means.

It is not unheard of for reporters to attempt to gain access to a center to interview families, or for lawyers to attempt entry to solicit business. Fortunately, this behavior is the exception, and disdained by all reputable members of both professions.

In all cases, the media should never be allowed access to the joint family assistance center. However, away from the center, family members can and often will talk to the media when they want to and no attempts should made to discourage or in any way hamper that contact.

As for attorneys, unsolicited visits should also be prohibited, however, family members should be allowed to bring their own attorneys with them and freely communicate with them when they wish.

If an unsolicited attorney or a media person is observed in the family assistance center, they should be quickly and quietly removed. Furthermore, they should be prosecuted to the fullest extent possible.

- **Coordinating daily information updates**—It has become routine for response agencies to conduct daily morning and evening briefings for the families on the various aspects of the incident response. Typically, the medical examiner, chief investigator, and any technical experts involved in the incident response will brief. The administration section should coordinate these daily information sessions and ensure that all family members are aware of their time and location.
- **Serving as a single point of contact for the family escorts or family members**—The final role of the administration section is to be a single contact point for all questions. Although the administration section cannot in all likelihood answer all questions, they should be able to find the right person and put them in contact with the family escort or family member. The goal here is to avoid having the family members feel that they are passed from one person to the next without ever getting a good answer. Remember that it is very hard to correct misinformation and family members will most likely not know from whom to get the right answer.

General Lounge Area

This needs to be nothing more than a common area, large enough to hold most of the family members. It should:

- Be accessible 24 hours a day
- Be only for the family members and escorts
- Have a television
- Have a separate children's area with childcare providers

Supervised Children's Area

Often families who come to the center will bring small children with them. However, during briefing and during the collection of antemortem information, the official notification process, or when making disposition, small children should not be present. Therefore, it will facilitate the process if a secure children's area staffed with qualified and trained childcare providers is available for the families' use.

Having specially trained grief counselors for children is a great thing to provide, but they should not talk with the children unless the parents have asked for or approved the communication.

Individual Family Briefing or Counseling Rooms

Several private rooms with comfortable furniture and telephones should be available for the collection of antemortem and disposition information, and the official notification of death.

Often, after receiving the official notification, family members will want to be alone to grieve and then possibly call other family members to let them know.

General Briefing Room

This should be an area large enough to accommodate all the family members at one time; you never want to conduct split briefings for the same audience as the information never comes out quite the same.

Considerations for setting up the briefing room are:

- Video link to other family assistance centers (if applicable)
- A side door through which the briefers can enter and leave
- A podium or raised area for the briefers
- Translators to translate the briefing
- Screen or chart board for use by the briefers
- Enough chairs for all family members to sit down

Typical Briefing Questions

1. **For the medical examiner:**
   - How many deceased have been recovered?
   - How long should the recovery take?
   - How many bodies have been positively identified?
   - How long should it take to positively identify everyone?
   - What is the condition of the bodies?
   - How many have been released?
   - How many people does the medical examiner have working?
   - How many hours a day is the medical examiner's operation running?
   - What resources does the medical examiner need that are missing?
   - What is happening with the personal effects?
   - When will the death certificates be issued?

2. **For the investigators:**
   - What is the status of any ongoing investigation?
   - Was the incident intentional, accidental, or an act of nature?
   - Did anyone have forewarning of the incident?
   - What agencies are working the incident?
   - How experienced are the investigators working the incident?
   - When can we visit the incident site?
   - How many people are investigating the incident?
   - When will the investigators have any answers?
   - What could have been done to save more people?

3. **For any industry involved in the incident:**
   - What are you doing about the incident?
   - What will you do to help take care of families?
   - Will you pay for funeral expenses?
   - Will you pay for (or continue to pay for) living expenses while we (families) are at the incident site?
   - What benefits will you provide to take of us?
   - Did you know that this incident could happen before it did?
   - How many employees, at what levels, were also killed?

These are only generalizations; not all questions will always be asked.

General Business Center

A small business center capable of supporting incoming facsimile machines, reproduction services, and word processing services is essential. Many documents will have to go between the joint family assistance center and the mass fatality morgue, and copies of legal documents, medical records, and other documents will undoubtedly be required.

Medical Assistance

On-site emergency medical care should be available, especially during the initial operations. Family members may suffer serious medical problems, emotionally distraught family members may need assistance or require basic care. I recommend having a team of emergency medical technicians and an ambulance at the center at all times.

Chapel—Interfaith Area

Finally, any Joint Family Assistance Center should have a small chapel and additional interfaith rooms set aside so that families can take solace in their own religious faiths. It is often said that one never meets an atheist during a battle; I believe the same thing could be said during a response to a mass fatality incident.

The chapel and interfaith rooms should be staffed by representatives of all predominant victims' faiths and points of contact for other faiths, available as needed.

Video Viewing Center

If possible, the joint family assistance center should be equipped with a video link to the morgue. A small private room with comfortable chairs should be set aside so if a family requests to view their relative they can do so through the use of video link. Naturally, the mass fatality incident morgue must also be equipped with a video link. If families ask and are able to view their lost family members, a grief counselor and appropriate religious representative should be present or close by if needed.

Other Considerations

- **Family Advocates**

Recently, families of transportation accidents and survivors of other incidents have formed legally recognized associations that often meet to discuss incident-specific issues as well as to further relationships that are often established among families and survivors. Additionally, these groups will lobby governments and industry for changes in safety standards to prevent future incidents and also to improve response standards. Some of these groups have become victim advocates and will often arrive at the scene of another mass fatality incident. Just like anything else, there are good and bad. During the incident response you will probably never hear of the good ones, because they focus on helping the families and the responders, not on speaking to the media. On the other hand, the ones to avoid will often be in front of the cameras.

The "good" advocates can provide invaluable assistance; they have been there and can truthfully say, "I know how you are feeling." The smart incident manager will listen to what advocates have to say, make use of their suggestions, and accept any offers to help.

- **Trips to the Incident Site**

Family members will often ask to visit the incident site. Every opportunity should be made to allow the families as a group to visit the incident site prior to any public access to the site. However, care should be taken to ensure that all remains and personal effects have first been recovered. As hard as it is to believe, family members have been allowed to go to incident sites where they found remains still present.

Figure 8.1 A newly established mass fatality incident memorial. Memorials such as this one are very important for most families, but some will want no mention of their loved ones on a memorial and will not want to participate in any ceremonies. (Courtesy of Kenyon International Services, Inc.)

- **Disposition of Unidentified Human Remains (Figure 1)**

The ME may decide that once all missing victims have been positively identified, the remaining fragments will not be identified. Once that decision is made, disposition of those fragments must be decided on. In previous incidents, the fragments have been placed into caskets and buried in a grave with all names in a marker or with no names. Again, the families should be consulted and their desires considered prior to any action.

- **Memorials (Figures 8.2, 8.3)**

Prior to the construction of any incident memorial, the families should be contacted and asked for their input. You will most likely not get full consensus on the design and placement of a memorial. However, it would be wise to go with the majority, and if some family members ask that their relatives' names not be included in a portion of the memorial, you should honor their wishes. Death and how it is managed is a very personal thing.

Figure 8.2 Family members and friends often establish their own memorials in accordance with their beliefs and customs. In any given mass fatality incident, the victims will most likely represent several distinct cultural groups. You should be sensitive to all of them. (Courtesy of Kenyon International Services, Inc.)

- **Resources**

As you have seen, taking care of families is resource intensive and requires very special people with a wide range of skills. As in other areas, I would not allow trainees or students, and would require that all personnel be over the age of 18, even the childcare providers. Consider the following the resources when establishing, operating, and maintaining a family assistance operations:

- Victim assistance counselors
- Professional grief counselors
- Various religious leaders
- Funeral directors
- Interpreters
- Red Cross
- Military casualty assistance personnel
- Plainclothes law enforcement
- Data entry personal
- Emergency medical technicians
- Specially trained phone operators
- Notary publics
- Legal counsel
- Trained childcare providers
- Janitorial or maintenance staff

Figure 8.3 Family members and friends gather at a mass fatality incident memorial to pay their resects. Today, in almost any mass fatality incident, you can expect that victims' families, friends, and also incident survivors will want to establish a memorial. (Courtesy of Kenyon International Services, Inc.)

Summary

I cannot overstress the importance of family assistance operations. Many businesses have learned the hard way that having an incident and paying all the associated costs, although not inexpensive, will most likely not put them out of business. However, not taking care of families properly will almost certainly guarantee a quick end to business. It is unfortunately a lesson that we seem to have to learn over and over. One only needs to look at the different aftermaths of some recent tragic events. Those in which the needs of the families were met are remembered with a sense of sadness for the victims but also a sense of pride for the support given to the families. On the other hand, some similar incidents are remembered not so much for the victims, but for the anguish over the manner in which the families were treated.

In short, the quality of your overall response will, in large part, be judged by your response to the families. This, as is most other areas in mass fatality incident management, is a zero-defect environment. Mistakes should not happen, but when they do, you cannot undo them. Therefore, it is critical to listen to the families, provide them with what you can, and do your best.

Media Operations

9

Once transmitted, images and words cannot be withdrawn or restated

In any mass fatality incident the media will converge on the incident site, the mass fatality incident morgue, the joint family assistance center, on the individual families when they can find them, and on responders (Figure 9.1).

The level of initial media response will depend on the type of incident and the location of occurrence. Mass fatality incidents that are part of a larger overall natural disaster such as an earthquake or hurricane will have less media attention just because it will likely be hard to get the media into the area and a greater focus will be placed on lifesaving and relief efforts.

Conversely, mass fatality incidents that are isolated incidents will receive all the focus. Furthermore, mass fatality incidents that occur in easily accessed areas will probably attract more and longer media visibility than an incident that occurs in a remote and possibly inhospitable climate. Another unfortunate reality is that the amount of coverage given to an incident will depend on what else is going on in the world. Also, any incident involving a celebrity or political leader will draw more attention.

But should the amount of media attention influence your response? The answer is, definitely not. The actions you take should be based on doing what is right regardless of who is watching. However, you must be prepared for the problems the media can cause and have the ability to solve those problems.

Media Response Issues – Potential Problems

Traditionally, the media response will range from professional factfinding and reporting to sensationalism. Media local to the incident site will not only understand the impact the incident has on the community, the victims'

Figure 9.1 Various media personnel will often seek responders for interviews. In this case, the president of a private response firm. (Courtesy of Kenyon International Emergency Services, Inc.)

families, survivors, and responders, but will also have time to present the full story. Non-local media may understand, but not actually appreciate, such community impact, and will most likely not have time to present the entire story.

Of course, in many cases, you can choose to ignore the media problems, but the end result of that can be very damaging to both the families and the reputation of the responders. It is better is to anticipate the problems and face them head on.

The most common issues or problems with media response are:

- **Presenting unverified information**—The result of this is many hours spent answering questions and tracking down the correct information—time that could be better spent managing response actions. Often the most common misinformation is (1) the total number of fatalities, either reported by "hearing" how many people are unaccounted for or looking at the total number of people who could possibly have been riding on a particular train; (2) the number of bodies recovered. Media personnel will watch the incident site, in fact, in previous incidents, they have gone so far as to rent apartments or houses close to the mass fatality incident morgue and sit and count how many human-remains pouches are brought into the morgue. You may recall from earlier chapters that each human-remains pouch does not necessarily equate to one complete person. However, many people in the media do not realize that, so they report that they have counted 100 fatalities being brought into the morgue, when the authorities are reporting only 81 people missing. Therefore, the perception is that someone is not telling the truth.

- **Questioning Response Actions**

While there is nothing wrong with asking why certain actions are occurring it is a mistake to blindly challenge a course of action without having an understanding of what should be happening. In countless incidents, the media have accused the medical examiner of not identifying the deceased quickly enough, yet few understand the requirements in establishing a positive identification.

- **Displaying Inappropriate Images**

Few things upset me more than to see a published picture or news video of a dead person at an incident site, even if the face of the person is unrecognizable. It bothers me because the images that the responders see should not be the ones the families see. If they want to see recovery photos, it should be when and where they want to see them, not when they turn on the television or open a magazine.

Although the majority of the media will take great pains to ensure that the faces of the deceased are not visible, the images are still disturbing. Case in point, after the Northridge earthquake in Southern California, a magazine published a rather large photo of a motorcycle policeman who had been killed during the earthquake. While you could only see his covered body and boots, that is the picture his family will most likely have as a last memory.

- **Asking Inappropriate Questions**

Without fail, whenever I am interviewed by the media about an incident I am asked, "What did the bodies look like?" I always decline to answer that question. I do so for the same reason that I don't approve of media pictures of the deceased.

As previously mentioned, remains recovered from a mass fatality incident are often fragmented and traumatized. Even with the knowledge that their loved one was dead before the actual fragmentation or other severe trauma occurred, the thought of the destruction done to the remains is something the families don't need. If the family wants to know the specifics, they should be told, but in person and privately.

- **Harassment of Family Members or Survivors**

Although many media agencies have taken great pains to protect the privacy of family members and not invade their lives, some agencies still insist on chasing family members and shoving cameras in their faces and asking them how they feel (Figure 9.2). Families should certainly have the right to speak with the media, but it should be at a time and place of their choosing, not just as they are finding out about the loss of someone who was dear to them.

Figure 9.2 Memorial services are another area in which you should expect media attention. Anticipating and planning for it will make it easier to manage. (Courtesy of Kenyon International Emergency Services, Inc.)

Media Response Issues – Potential Benefits

As with most everything else in life there are benefits along with the negatives. In the case of the media, there are several potential benefits.

- Requests for information—The media can aid responders in disseminating information. For mass fatality incidents involving large public buildings, places, or transportation where passenger manifests are not created such as on ferries or mass transportation, the media can publish telephone numbers for people to report missing family or friends who might have been involved in the incident. They can also ask the public to contact family and friends who they think might have been involved and if they cannot contact them, to then telephone the call center.

- **Requests for additional manpower, supplies, or equipment**—The media can also assist by appealing for specialized help during mass fatality incidents, especially those that occur as part of a larger disaster. This is also true for requesting specialized equipment or needed supplies. Given the opportunity to help during a mass fatality incident most people will jump at the chance to be part of the response. The challenge is to get the right resources at the right time; the media can help you do that.

- **Area closure / evacuation information**—Rarely do mass fatality incidents occur in areas that do not affect the daily movement of people in and out of a given area. Often the incident area may be closed to the public for weeks and even months. The public should be alerted to the closure of certain areas and the effect the closure will have on day-to-day activities. The easiest way to do this is through mass media announcements. Unfortunately, announcing that an area is closed will also inadvertently serve as an invitation to some curiosity seekers. To the best of my knowledge, no one has been able to come up with a solution for that.

- **Pressure government agencies to increase response actions**—In some mass fatality incidents, responding agencies have been determined to manage the incident as if nothing extraordinary had occurred. In other words, they refuse all offers of outside help; they operate within normal hours and with normal staffing; and they expect that people's reactions will be no different from reactions to deaths that occur from natural causes. In these cases, the media can play a great role for the families or for those responders who know that things should be different. Groups of families, justifiably complaining about the response, via the media can bring unfavorable attention to those individuals who are in a position to influence the response and change it for the better. In fact, many laws, both good and bad, have been enacted because of the attention raised by rightfully outraged family members and incident survivors.

Managing the Media Response

Two things you can do to help successfully manage the media response:

1. Appoint a designated media spokesperson
2. Establish, operate, and maintain a joint information center

Designated Media Spokesperson

During the incident response the single most important thing your agency can do to manage the incident is to have a trained designated media- or press-information spokesperson. Each response agency should have such a person; but, during joint response operations, the primary or lead agency for the current phase of the operation should have the lead spokesperson.

Spokespersons should have a complete understanding of the operational response. They should be experienced, and hopefully have a positive established relationship with local media. They will be crucial to the way the response is portrayed. Their responsibilities are:

- Keep the media informed
- Schedule press briefings
- Provide written new releases
- Serve as single point of contact
- Recommend areas for press filming or providing pool footage
- Advise the incident commander on media activities

The Joint Information Center

Another tool for managing the media response is to establish a joint information center. The word "joint" is added because many organizations will play a key role in the establishment, operation, and maintenance of the center. Representatives of the various response agencies should be available at the joint information center or when requested by the center.

The purpose of a joint information center is to provide:

- A central location for regularly scheduled press information briefs
- A location where all agency spokespersons can work and be readily available for media inquiries
- A place for media to gather to wait for more information
- An area for appropriate agency heads to be interviewed

The lead agency to establish the joint information center should be the agency initially responsible for handling the incident.

Establishment of a Joint Information Center

Within hours after a mass fatality incident has occurred the lead responding agency should began establishing the joint information center. Because the cost of establishing a center will be almost entirely borne by government agencies, existing facilities should be considered. In some cases, facilities might consist of large mobile vans or trailers.

Joint Information Center Considerations

Once the decision has been made, the next thing to think of is where the center should be established, which must be decided on rapidly. Considerations for this are:

- Is the facility available immediately? In most cases, the media will arrive on scene within hours of the responders. In some cases, they may actually beat a large percentage of responders to the scene.
- Is it available for as long as needed? For planning purposes I would expect the center to operate for as long as any search and recovery of remains and personal effects is ongoing.
- Does it have controlled access? Only accredited media personnel should be allowed access.
- Does the facility have the basics, water, sewer, electrical power, ventilation, and climate control? Can the telephone and data transmission capabilities be rapidly expanded?
- Is it arranged to facilitate proper press briefings? It should have a large enough area to allow all media to fit into the briefing room. It should also be set up so that briefers can enter and leave the area without having to make their way through the media to get in and out.
- Is the facility close enough to the incident site? The medical examiner and other responders should be able to travel relatively easily between the site and the center to conduct briefings, yet the facility should be far enough away from the joint family assistance center to protect the families.
- Is the facility disability friendly? People who have physical handicaps should be able to easily access the facility and use the amenities provided.

Joint Information Center Layout

The joint information center should be organized to accommodate the following operational sections:

- Reception station
- Large briefing room
- Large lounge or break room
- Business and communications center

Reception Station

The reception station plays many key roles. It is responsible for:

Controlling access to the center.   This can be a difficult process. All media personnel should have an agency photo identification.

Maintaining the database.   A simple database of who has come to the center and any of their contact information should be collected and maintained.

Maintaining printed press releases.   Any releases provided to the media should be noted and copies kept. Additionally, during the time the joint information center is operational, copies of any printed releases should always be available.

Coordinating security.   All security issues and concerns should be managed by this section. Personnel should coordinate shift changes and ensure that the proper authorities are notified whenever there are any problems. Uniformed law enforcement should be present in the area to ensure only authorized media members gain access and to assist in resolving any problems.

Coordinating daily information updates.   It has become routine for response agencies to conduct daily morning and evening briefings on the various aspects of the incident response for the media. Typically, the medical examiner, chief investigator, and any technical experts involved in the incident response will brief. The reception section should coordinate these daily briefings and ensure that the times and locations are posted and known to all.

- Serve as a single point of contact for information—The final role of the reception station is to be a single point for all questions. Although the reception section may not be able to answer all questions, they should be able to find the right person who can. The goal here is to avoid having the media feeling that they are passed from one person to the next without ever getting a good answer. Remember that it is very hard to correct misinformation and the media will most likely not know who to get the right answer from.

General Briefing Room

This should be an area large enough to accommodate all media members at once. You never want to conduct split briefings for the same audience, as the information never comes out the same way twice.

Considerations are:

- A side door for the briefers to enter and leave by
- A podium or raised area for the briefers
- Translators to translate the briefing
- Screen or chart board for use by the briefers
- Enough chairs for all attendees to sit down
- Enough raised spaces for cameras and microphones

Typical Media Questions

1. **For the medical examiner:**
   - How many bodies have been recovered?
   - How long should the recovery take?
   - How many families have been contacted?
   - How many bodies have been positively identified?
   - How long should it take to positively identify all the fatalities?
   - What is the condition of the bodies?
   - What types of injuries do the victims have?
   - How many bodies have been released?
   - What experience does the ME have?
   - How many people does the ME have working?
   - How many hours a day is the ME's operation running?
   - What resources does the ME need that are not available?
   - What is happening with the personal effects?
   - What outside agencies are involved?
   - How does the response process work?

2. **For the investigators:**
   - What is the status of any ongoing investigation?
   - Was the incident intentional, accidental, or an act of nature?
   - Did anyone have forewarning of the incident?
   - What agencies are working the incident?
   - How experienced are the investigators working the incident?
   - When can we visit the incident site?
   - How many people are investigating the incident?
   - When will the investigators have any answers?
   - What could have been done to save more people?

3. **For any industry involved in the incident:**
   - What are you doing about the incident?

- Is there any danger of this type of incident happening somewhere else?
- What are you doing to help take care of families?
- What expenses will you pay for?
- How many families are here?
- Will you pay for or continue to pay for living expenses while families are at the incident site?
- What long-term benefits will you provide to care for the families?
- Did you know that this incident could happen before it did?
- How many of those who were killed were employees?
- If any employees were killed, what were their jobs?

Most of these questions are the same or similar to those that the families will ask. As always, depending on the incident, different questions may be asked.

General Lounge Area

This needs to be nothing more than a common area large enough to hold a good portion of the media. Obviously it is not a requirement to have a lounge, but I always think that if I can provide a comfortable area where information will always be released first, then perhaps I can encourage people to remain there and wait as opposed to going to the site or the morgue and getting in the way. Suggestions for the lounge area are:

- Be accessible 24 hours a day
- Have several desks or writing areas
- Have a television
- Have vending machines or coffee and soda available

General Business and Communication Center

A business center capable of supporting incoming facsimile machines, reproduction services, and word processing services is also a nice touch.

Additional Media Considerations

In addition to having a designated media spokesperson and establishing, operating, and maintaining a joint information center, agency leaders should consider the following supplementary management steps:

- **Declare the incident site a biohazard area or crime scene**—Although the decision to declare an area a crime scene or biohazard area should be not done to exclude media coverage, it can, in fact, mean that the media—or many others for that matter—will be restricted from gaining access to the site, because, while the media are still legally allowed access to a crime scene, they are often not allowed access to a biohazard area. Usually the local health service agency has the authority to declare a site a biohazard and close access to it.

- **Restrict media access to all areas except the joint information center**—As stated in previous chapters, many areas of the incident response, and especially the incident site, mass fatality incident morgue, and joint family assistance center, should be restricted from media access.

- **Provide pool footage**—If you restrict access to the incident site, consider using pool footage. One agency's professional media services unit should shoot the footage. Key points to remember are:
    1. Shoot selectively—as we mentioned, certain things should not be shown.
    2. Keep in mind the media's requirements, and shoot the footage from the cameraman's or editor's perspective.
    3. Focus on all areas of the response and all agencies responding.
    4. Edit the tape before releasing it.
    5. Make the footage available to everyone at the same time.

- **Immediately provide preprinted information sheets**—Because mass fatality incidents are not an everyday occurrence for most agencies, information about how the response should or will go is not common to many people; reporters are no exception. During the initial stages of the response effort you will probably not have time to write up information sheets. Therefore, I suggest that as part of your preplanning process all agencies potentially involved in a incident response should prepare and maintain information sheets that are readily available for immediate distribution after an incident occurs.

Preprinted information sheets should include:

1. Explanation of operational flow
2. Definitions of terms such as:
    - Positive identification
    - Tentative identification
    - Associated personal effects
    - Unassociated personal effects
3. The role of each response agency

4. The role of outside agencies that might be expected to participate
5. The organization and role of certain operational areas such as:
   - Mass Fatality Incident Morgue
   - Personal Effects Warehouse
   - Joint Family Assistance Center
   - Joint Information Center
   - Joint Logistics Support Center

- Do everything possible to protect families from the media—Certainly do not take any action to prevent those families who wish to contact the media from doing so. However, let it be the choice of the families, not the media.

Some Basic Media Pointers

- *Understand the role of reporters.* Take the attitude that the reporter represents the public and that you want the public to know your story
- *Know your subject.* Anticipate questions you will be asked. Be prepared, and have the most current information.
- *Know what you want to say.* Have main ideas, facts, and figures. They should be updated and readily available every time you brief. State them up front and repeat them for emphasis.
- *Relate your answers to the reader, not the reporter.* What do readers expect to read? What do they want to read? What should they read?
- *Be brief.* Give short, to-the-point answers. State your conclusions, then provide supporting material.
- *Be positive.* Turn negative questions into positive ones and don't dwell on the negative.
- *Use conversational language.* Use words and phrases that the public understands, not technical terms, acronyms, or abbreviations.
- *Answer the question asked.* Don't try to be evasive, answer the question in your terms, not the reporter's. If you can't or don't want to answer the question, say so and explain why. If you don't know, say so, and offer to find the answer or someone who can. Give definite answers.
- *Don't accept a reporter's facts, figures, or terminology.* Don't use a reporter's words or let them put words in your mouth. If a reporter is wrong, provide the correct answer.
- *Don't answer hypothetical questions.* Don't speculate, answer with what is current and not what *might* happen.
- *Practice answering difficult questions.* Be prepared for hard questions, know the skeletons in the closet.

- *Never comment off the record.* Expect that anything you say will appear in print.
- *Don't lie.* Lies always come back and make everything else you say or do suspect. Be honest and factual—if you make a mistake, admit it.

Summary

I cannot overemphasize the importance of good media-management operations. Many government agencies and businesses have learned the hard way that no matter how well they managed the response to an incident, if the media coverage is unfavorable, the perception will be that they did a poor job. In some cases, the media coverage can be enough to call for agency heads to be removed or businesses to fail. It does not have to be this way. Unfortunately, this is a lesson that seems to be difficult to learn.

Having a good media-management plan is also something that does not just happen. Like most areas, pre-incident coordination is key, as well as having trained spokespersons who can get along with the media and understand the media's role.

In short, the quality of your response will in large part be judged by the public's perception of your actions. This, as in most other areas in mass fatality incident management, is a zero-defect environment. Although in media management mistakes happen, they can be hard to correct.

Logistical Support Operations

10

Total support for total resolution

Logistics is the process of planning for, requesting, receiving, distribution, use, sustainment, and turn-in, of facilities, food, beverages, equipment, and supplies (Figure 10.1). In this guide I will also include personnel-support needs.

In the large majority of mass fatality incidents, support for the response operations will come from the responding agencies and although accelerated, will probably not be that much different from day-to-day support operations. However, in the remaining percentage of incidents, a complete support system for personnel, supplies, and equipment could be required.

In the initial response stages of a mass fatality incident agency leaders will need to make a determination whether routine support channels will be sufficient for the operational response. If it is insufficient, a logistical support area should be established.

If a logistical support area is deemed necessary, a primary or lead agency should be selected to establish, operate, and maintain the area. If the mass fatality incident is so large that it requires a logistical support area, an agency that has not yet been tasked should be picked to be the primary or lead agency. Agencies such as local roads, parks, or services departments are probably very well suited in that they most likely deal with the management of resources and resource replenishment on a daily basis. Additionally, they are also less likely to be affected by the mass fatality incident response.

Naturally, other response agencies should send representatives who have the authority to order things for that operational area, and, more important, have the knowledge of what is needed so that they can anticipate requirements and begin to fill them immediately.

Figure 10.1   Empty coffins being off-loaded at a mass fatality incident morgue. Note that they were transported in a covered vehicle. (Courtesy of Kenyon International Emergency Services, Inc.)

Establishment of a Logistical Support Area

A logistical support area assists all operations. Its primary functions are to:

- Serve as the incident staging area
- Coordinate volunteer activities
- Receive and redirect all volunteers, equipment, supplies, and services
- Manage and monitor all financial actions
- Serve as a single point of contact for requesting, receiving, and utilization of facilities, equipment, supplies, and services.

The logistical support area should be established as soon as possible after the incident and it should be prepared to support the following operational areas:

- Incident management operations center
- Security operations
- Search and recovery operations
- Mass fatality incident morgue
- Personal effects operations
- Joint family assistance center

- Joint information center
- Logistics support area (self support)

Logistical Facility Considerations

Once the decision to establish a logistical support area has been made, the next thing to consider is where to establish the operation. Considerations for this are:

- Is the facility available for the long term? Large resource-intensive incidents can last for months. In some recent cases, active support operations continued well over six months after a major incident.
- Does it have enough access to allow for the delivery and shipment of supplies and equipment?
- Does the facility have the basics—water, sewer, electrical power, ventilation, and climate control?
- Is the facility single story and does it have an access door that can accommodate material-handling equipment such as pallet jacks and small forklifts? If you use a multistory building, it should have a heavy-duty lift or elevator.
- Does the facility have space for working offices as well as an area for the breakdown and distribution of equipment and supplies?
- Is the facility located far enough from the incident site, joint family assistance center and mass fatality incident morgue to be outside any security perimeter, yet be a reasonable distance to those activities? Access to the logistical support facility should be open to the public.

The decision to establish a logistical support facility should be made early on. Once that decision is made and the operation established, all requests for support and all responding personnel and equipment should report there.

Logistical Support Area Layout

The typical logistical support area will contain the following areas and stations:

- Administration
- Supply and equipment warehouse
    - a. Receiving
    - b. Distribution
- Services
- Personnel

Administration Station

The administration station plays many key roles. It is responsible for

Controls access to certain areas.   Although access to the area should be open to the public, certain areas need to be restricted. Areas with supplies or material-handling equipment should be closed to the public except when they are dropping off supplies or equipment.

Maintains a database.   A simple system recording items requested by each operational area, the requisition, the purchasing or donation, and finally the distribution of those items should be maintained and accessible to the people staffing the logistical support area.

Coordinates security.   All security issues and concerns should be managed by this section, which should coordinate shift changes and ensure that the proper authorities are notified whenever there are any problems. Uniformed law enforcement should be present in the area to ensure that items are not stolen or used inappropriately.

Serves as the accounting section.   The type of incident will often determine who will be expected to pay for what. However, that determination may not be made until well into the incident response. Support operations can frequently not wait for that determination, therefore, it is important that all costs are tracked and expenditures accounted for. When and if reimbursement is later forthcoming, it can be applied to the proper locations.

   Ideally, a designated person in the requesting organization should approve all requests received and the signature authorizing the request should acknowledge agency responsibility to pay for the requested items.

Serve as a single point of contact.   The final role of the administration section is to serve as a single point of contact for all support requests. Any request for support should go through the operational area chain of command and then be forwarded through the operational agency's representative to the logistical support area, where the request is acted on.

   Inquiries from the public about what and how many items are needed should be directed to the logistical support area. The goal here is to consolidate needs and ensure that all requirements are being filled, as well as tracking the cost of response.

   The goal here is to consolidate needs and ensure that all requirements are being filled, as well as tracking the cost of response.

Supply and Equipment Warehouse

The supply and equipment warehouse is the part of the logistical support area that actually receives supplies and equipment and then distributes them to operational areas as needed (Figure 10.2). It is divided into two stations: receiving and distribution.

Figure 10.2   Various pieces of equipment displayed from a mass fatality incident morgue kit. Note the storage and shipping boxes. (Courtesy of Kenyon International Emergency Services, Inc.)

- **Receiving Station**

As supplies or equipment are brought to the logistical support area the receiving section should:

1. Inventory the items and ensure that they match what was ordered.
2. Check that the items are serviceable.
3. Issue a receipt for the orders.
4. Forward a copy of the receiving document to the administration section.
5. Forward the items to the distribution station or, if busy, storage stations.
6. Forward copies of any documentation to the administrative section.

- **Distribution Station**

Here the supplies or equipment are prepared for pickup by the requesting agency. Specific actions are:

1. Take possession of the items from receiving.

2. Determine what operational facility they go to.
3. Contact the receiving operational facility representative and advise what items are ready for pick-up.
4. Prepare a receiving document.
5. Place the items into organized storage areas.
6. Once the items have been picked up and signed for, copies of any paperwork should be forwarded to the administration station.

Services

In addition to the supply and equipment needs, responding agencies will most likely also have recurring service needs that are usually best filled with short-term contingency contracts or by getting service support from outside the affected area. Typical services required are:

- Communications
- Food and beverage
- Billeting
- General facilities
- Sanitary services
- Medical
- Transportation

Communications

The ability to communicate during a mass fatality incident is critical. While some of the larger response agencies may have enough radios and cellular phones for internal communications, smaller agencies will not and additional resources will be required to enable agencies to communicate with one another.

To facilitate this, the service section of the logistical support area should acquire as many secure portable radios, radio frequencies, cellular phones, pagers, and some International Maritime Satellite Phones (INMARSAT) as is possible.

Also, the international group, the Military Affiliated Radio Stations (MARS), a group of civilian "ham" radio operators who operator and maintain their own equipment can prove invaluable. In many disasters, they have responded and established communications when no other means were available or possible.

Some Key Things to Remember

- Many government agencies have a cache of communication devices available for emergency use; they must simply be requested.
- Many government agencies also have a certain number of radio frequencies or channels identified for use only as emergency channels; again, they are available for the asking.
- Cellular phones may not work in all areas. If the mass fatality incident is part of a natural disaster such as an earthquake in which land mass has shifted, the cell phones will probably not work, as the cell towers were most likely knocked out of alignment.
- Cellular phones can be easily monitored, and therefore sensitive information should not be discussed over them.
- The media will often get a cellular line and leave it open to ensure that they have instant communications.
- INMARSAT will work almost anywhere but is very costly.
- Not everyone involved in an incident needs a communication device. Too many responders with access to devices can easily overload and shut down a system.
- Support contracts for the daily replacement or charging of batteries should also be considered

Food and Beverage Service

The food and beverage section should arrange for the procurement of meals and beverages. This service should also include delivery to the operational areas, except for the joint family assistance center, which should be close to restaurants.

A contract service is the best way to provide this support.

Key points to remember:

- If operations are ongoing 24 hours a day, food and beverage service should be available also. Delivery of food and beverages should be scheduled to allow for four main meals, and snacks available at most times.
- Beverage service should include individually bottled water, soft drinks, and coffee and tea.
- Meal choice should be sensitive to the incident. In other words, barbecue should not be served at a mass fatality fire incident or seafood at a water recovery site.

Billeting

Depending on the size of the incident and the number of responders coming from outside the local area, billeting or lodging resources may be required.

Although tents will suffice in some situations, the better answer is individual hotel rooms. Ideally, responders should be billeted at a location separate from the joint family assistance center. This is to allow them the opportunity to unwind and talk over the day's activities. Certainly all responders should be cautioned to be careful about what they say in public. As mentioned earlier, the media may go to the areas where the responders rest and congregate.

If you cannot arrange for a large enough facility to billet the majority of responders, at least keep individuals from the same agency together.

General Facilities

If government facilities were not available or were used for another center, then contracts for the lease or rental of those facilities should be maintained by this section. Although the facilities may have been acquired before the establishment and operation of the logistical support area, once the support area is fully functional, oversight and management of the contract should be under the control of this station.

Sanitary Services

Local contracts should also be considered for the renting and servicing of portable latrine facilities. These facilities should be placed near the various operational areas and serviced daily.

Medical

Medical services should be provided for the responders. Many well-developed response teams will have their own medical support to include the mental health programs discussed at length in Chapter 3. If the response team arrives without medical and mental health support, or do not have organic resources, the following services should be provided:

- Daily monitoring of work areas to ensure proper fluid intake, and use of personnel protective equipment
- Immediate emergency medical care for injuries
- Vaccinations if needed
- Post-exposure treatment for occupational exposure to bloodborne pathogens or hazardous materials
- Immediate mental health services if needed

Transportation

Although many response agencies will arrive with their own transportation resources, an equal number will not.

Upon establishment of a logistical supply area, a collection of local government vehicles to include cars, vans, buses, and light, medium, and heavy trucks should be acquired. If these types of vehicles are unavailable, rental vehicles should be considered. After billeting, rental cars are often the next thing to become rapidly unavailable in a local area following a mass fatality incident.

Each operational area should sign for and provide their own drivers for the vehicles. Similarly, a central fueling station or credit card should be provided so that proper cost accounting can be tracked.

Personnel

The personnel section of the logistical support area serves a very important function. Once the logistical support area is established all personnel responding to the incident should process through this area.

The specific function of the personnel section is to:

- Direct personnel to the right location
- Issue any required security access badges
- Coordinate request and distribution of volunteers
- Verify, if required, volunteers' credentials or licenses
- Track responder data, which should include who is on scene, when they arrived, what agency they belong to, any injuries they may have suffered, and when they leave the site
- Provide daily personnel totals to the administration station

Logistical Resources

Many personnel who want to help but who are not suitable for any other response area are perfect for the logistical support area. Consideration should be given to people with a background in:

- Inventory control
- Receiving, shipping, and transportation experience
- Accounting

- Communications
- Medical technicians
- Preventive health specialists
- Database management
- Business owners

Specific agency resources to consider, including technical or agency representatives, are the following:

- Sworn law enforcement
- Fire department
- Medical examiner administrator
- Local parks and recreation managers
- Local mass transit managers
- Local procurement managers
- Military
- General services administration
- Government procurement officers

Summary

As in most major operations, logistics is often the most forgotten planning aspect. In a majority of incidents, a major logistical support area will not be required. However, if one is required it should be immediately established and it should support all operational areas. A well-run support operation can ensure that the right items and people get to the right area with a minimum of delay. It can make accounting for items easy and therefore reimbursement requests simple.

More important, to ensure proper follow up, a good support operation can ensure that response personnel are properly vaccinated and have the right credentials, and track any injuries or problems they might have.

However, good logistical support operations don't just happen; like everything else we have discussed, plans must be made in advance and certain agreements and understanding reached. Unfortunately, many incident responders make the mistake of taking for granted that they always have what they need and whatever they need will just be there. Don't fall into that trap—plan ahead.

Federal Response Resources 11

Although the majority of this guide is intended for use in any part of the world, this chapter deals specifically with the Federal Response resources of the Federal Government of the USA, which are possibly unique to this country and may not apply to other countries' national response structure.

For many years, the federal response to disasters and mass fatality incidents was haphazard and generally resulted in too little help too late. That response changed greatly in 1988, when Public Law 93-288 was amended by Public Law 100-707 and retitled the Robert T. Stafford Disaster Relief and Emergency Act (Public Law 93-288, as amended).

As a result of the Stafford Act, the Federal Response Plan was created, and frankly, it is a very good plan. The Federal Emergency Management Agency (FEMA), which maintains the plan, has done an outstanding job with its development and, on many occasions, its execution. If it has any faults, it is that many in the lower levels of government lack knowledge of the plan and how it works.

The Federal Response Plan

The plan describes the basic mechanisms and structure by which the federal government will mobilize resources and conduct activities to augment state and local response efforts. The plan uses a functional approach to group the types of federal assistance a state is most likely to need under 12 Emergency Support Functions (ESFs). Each ESF is headed by a primary agency that has been selected based on its resources and capabilities in the particular functional area. Other agencies have been designated as support agencies for one or more ESFs based on their resources and capabilities to support the functional area. The 12 ESFs serve as the primary mechanism through which federal response assistance will be provided to assist the state in meeting response requirements in an affected area. (Lead and primary agencies are shown in matrix in Figure 11.1.)

Additionally, the plan assigns specific functional responsibilities, identifies actions required by participating federal departments, and applies to all federal agencies tasked by the plan.

FEMA has organized support for the plan based on the regional concept. FEMA has divided the U.S. into 10 different operational regions, each with a headquarters.

Some key points of the plan:

The President may declare an emergency with or without a Governor's request, as specified in Title V of Public Law 93-288, as amended (the Robert T. Stafford Disaster Relief and Emergency Act.) Under Title V, the President may direct the provision of emergency assistance, either at the request of a Governor or upon determination by the President that an "emergency exists for which the primary responsibility for response rests with the United States."

The American Red Cross (ARC) is deemed to be a federal agency for the purposes of the plan. Though created by the U.S. Congress in 1905, the ARC is a private, charitable corporation whose primary functions include the alleviation of human suffering caused by disaster or other natural catastrophe.

A federal agency or designated employee of a federal agency, including the American Red Cross (ARC) and its employees and volunteers, performing a function under the authority of Public Law 93-288, as amended, are not liable for any claim based upon the exercise or performance of or the failure to exercise or perform that function.

The plan is organized as follows:

- **Basic plan**—Covers the purpose, scope, situation, policies, and concept of operations of federal response activity in a disaster.
- **Appendices**—Includes a list of acronyms and abbreviations, terms and definitions, and authorities and directives.
- **Functional annexes**—Describe the policies, situation, planning assumptions, concept of operations, and responsibilities for each ESF.
- **Support Annexes**—Describe the areas of financial management, public information, and congressional relations.

FEMA Organization

National Level:

- **Catastrophic Disaster Response Group (CDRG)**

A national headquarters-level coordinating group composed of representatives of the 27 federal departments and agencies that have responsibilities

ESF #	1 TRANSPORTATION	2 COMMUNICATIONS	3 PUBLIC WORKS AND ENGINEERING	4 FIREFIGHTING	5 INFORMATION & PLANNING	6 MASS CARE	7 RESOURCE SUPPORT	8 HEALTH & MEDICAL SUPPORT	9 URBAN SEARCH & RESCUE	10 HAZARDOUS MATERIALS	11 FOOD	12 ENERGY
USDA	S	S	S	P	S	S	S	S	S	S	P	S
DOC		S	S		S	S	S	S		S		
DOD	S	S	P	S	S	S	S	S	S	S	S	S
DOEd					S							
DOE	S		S		S		S	S		S		P
DHHS			S		S	S	S	P	S	S	S	
DHUD					S							
DOI		S	S	S	S					S		
DOJ					S			S		S		
DOL			S				S		S	S		
DOS	S									S		S
DOT	P	S	S		S	S	S	S	S	S	S	S
TREAS					S							
VA			S			S	S	S				
AID								S	S			
ARC					S	P		S			S	
EPA		S	S		S			S	S	P	S	
FCC		S										
FEMA		S		S	P	S	S	S	P	S	S	
GSA	S	S	S		S	S	P	S	S	S		S
ICC	S											
NASA					S							
NCS		P			S			S	S			S
NRC					S					S		S
OPM							S					
SBA					S							
TVA	S		S									S
USPS	S					S		S				

Chart was taken, with slight modification, from the Federal Response Plan (for Public Law 93-288, As Amended) April 1992

Figure 11.1 Matrix chart of the various U.S. federal agencies and the areas of the U.S. Federal Response Plan they support.

under the plan. The FEMA associate director (State and Local Programs and Support Directorate) chairs the CDRG.

- **Emergency Support Team (EST)**

An interagency group composed of representatives from each of the primary agencies, select support agencies, and FEMA headquarters staff.

Listing of acronyms used in the Emergency Support Function Matrix.

USDA	United States Department of Agriculture
DOC	Department of Commerce
DOD	Department of Defense
DOEd	Department of Education
DHHS	Department of Health and Human Services
DHUD	Department of Housing and Urban Development
DOI	Department of the Interior
DOJ	Department of Justice
DOL	Department of Labor
DOS	Department of State
DOT	Department of Transportation
TREAS	Department of Treasury
VA	Department of Veterans Affairs
AID	Agency for International Development
ARC	American Red Cross
EPA	Environmental Protection Agency
FCC	Federal Communications Commission
FEMA	Federal Emergency Management Agency
GSA	General Services Administration
ICC	Interstate Commerce Commission
NASA	National Aeronautics and Space Administration
NCS	National Communications System
NRC	Nuclear Regulatory Commission
OPM	Office of Personal Management
SBA	Small Business Administration
TVA	Tennessee Valley Authority
USPS	United States Postal Service

Please note that for the purposes of the Federal Response Plan (FRP) the American Red Cross is considered a government agency.

Figure 11.1   (Continued).

• Emergency Support Function Emergency Operations Centers
Nothing more than national level emergency operations centers for each of the 27 federal agencies involved in supporting the plan.

Regional Levels

• **Emergency Response Team (ERT)**
An interagency group that provides administrative, logistical, and operational support to the regional response activities in the field. The ERT includes staff from FEMA and other agencies. Each FEMA regional office is responsible for rostering an ERT and developing appropriate procedures for notification and deployment.
Each ERT also includes:

- **Administration and Logistics Group**
Includes activities that provide facilities and services in support of response operations, as well as for recovery activities. Includes the disaster field office support functions of administrative services, fiscal services, computer support, and a message center.

    a. *Information and Planning Group (ESF 5)*—Includes information and planning activities to support operations. It includes functions to collect and process information; develop information into briefings, reports, and other materials; display pertinent information on maps, charts and status boards; consolidate information for action planning; and provide technical services in the from of advice on specialized areas of support operations.

    b. *Response Operations*—Representatives from the ESFs that will be deployed.

    c. *Recovery Operations*—This element includes the program activities of FEMA and other federal agencies that provide disaster recovery assistance.

Key Players

- **Emergency Response Team Advance (ERT-A)**—The ERT-A is the advance team of the ERT. It is the nucleus of the entire ERT.

- **Federal Coordinating Officer (FCO)**—As the senior federal official appointed in accordance with the provisions of the Robert T. Stafford Disaster Relief and Emergency Act (Public Law 93-288, as amended), the FCO represents the President. Additionally, the FCO is delegated responsibilities and performs those for the FEMA director and regional director.

- **Defense Coordinating Officer (DCO)**—A military or civilian Department of Defense (DOD) official specifically designated to mediate DOD support activity. As the DOD's designated on-scene member of the ERT, the DCO is the single point of contact for coordinating and tasking the use of all DOD resources.

- **Disaster Field Office (DFO)**—The office established in or near the designated area to support federal and state response and recovery operations. The DFO houses the FCO and the ERT, and, where possible, the state coordinating officer and support staff.

- **Regional Operations Center (ROC)**—The temporary operations facility for the coordination of federal response and recovery activities located at the FEMA regional office and led by the FEMA regional director or deputy director until the DFO becomes operational.

- **State Coordinating Officer (SCO)**—The representative of the Governor, who coordinates state, commonwealth, or territorial response and recovery activities with those of the federal government.

Response Sequence

Notification of an Incident

- FEMA receives the initial notification or warning of a disaster. FEMA can receive this notification from multiple sources such as state emergency operations centers, other federal agencies, or the media.
- Upon determination of the disaster or need to implement the plan, the FEMA National Emergency Coordination Center (NECC) will notify key FEMA headquarters and regional personnel. If there is a need for activation of response structures of the plan, the NECC will notify the Catastrophic Disaster Response Group (CDRG), a national headquarters-level coordinating group composed of representatives of the 27 federal departments and agencies that have responsibilities under the plan. The FEMA associate director chairs the CDRG. The NECC will also notify the Emergency Support Team, which is an interagency group composed of representatives from each of the primary agencies, select support agencies, and FEMA headquarters staff.
- At the regional level, the appropriate regional director will notify members of the Emergency Response Teams (ERT), which is the interagency group that provides administrative, logistical, and operational support to the regional response activities in the field. The ERT includes staff from FEMA and other agencies. Each FEMA regional office is responsible for rostering an ERT and developing appropriate procedures for notification and deployment.
- Upon notification by FEMA, each agency is responsible for conducting its own internal national and regional notifications.
- CDRG members may be called to assemble at the FEMA Emergency Information and Coordination Center for an initial meeting. CDRG members or their designated representatives must be available at the call of the CDRG chairperson to meet any time during the initial response period or as necessary.

Activation of The Plan

- The plan will be utilized to address particular requirements of a given disaster. Selected Emergency Support Functions will be activated based

on the nature and scope of the event and level of federal resources required to support the state and local resources.
- Once a response requirement is identified, some or all of the structures of the plan will be activated. This includes the establishment of the Emergency Support Team at headquarters level, the activation of some or all of the ESFs and the deployment of an ERT from the regional office.
- At the national level, the FEMA associate director, in consultation with the FEMA director, has the authority to activate part or all of the response structures at the headquarters level to address the specific situation.
- At the regional level, a FEMA regional director, in consultation with the associate director and the FEMA director also may activate part or all of the response structures of the plan within the region for the purpose of providing response support to an affected state.
- Based on the requirements of the situation, FEMA headquarters and regional offices will notify federal departments and agencies regarding activation of some or all of the ESFs and other structures of the plan.

FEMA Response Actions

FEMA Headquarters Actions

- The FEMA director will provide information on the requirements for federal response assistance to the White House and to senior-level federal government officials, as required. The EST and CDRG will convene as appropriate.
- The interagency EST will assemble at FEMA within two hours of notification to begin operations.
- At the call of the CDRG chairperson, the CDRG will convene. Members will report on their agency deployment actions and initial activities in support of the ESFs.

FEMA Regional Actions

- Upon occurrence of an event that requires or may require a federal response, the FEMA regional director will initiate federal response activities from the regional office.
- FEMA and other federal agencies will activate their regional operations centers and establish links with the affected state(s) until the ERT is established in the field.

- The FEMA regional director, with the support of the ESFs, will initially deploy members of the ERT advance team, commonly referred to as the ERT-A, to the affected state(s) for the purpose of assessing the impact of the situation, collecting damage information, and determining response requirements. The regional director will coordinate the federal support of state(s) requirements until the FCO assumes those responsibilities.

Federal Response Operational Flow

1. Before a federal disaster declaration:

- FEMA regional director dispatches ERT-A
- FEMA regional director activates ESF
- FEMA regional director confers with the ERT-A and state officials to determine the state's needs.

2. After the federal disaster declaration:

- Disaster field office is established
- The complete ERT arrives
- The federal coordinating officer, defense coordinating officer, and state coordinating officer are all appointed.
- Various emergency support functions are activated and primary and supporting agencies start arriving.

Obviously a lot of coordination and discussion among different federal agencies and the affected state(s) must occur, but in previous incidents the coordination has gone surprisingly well and the operation has come together smoothly.

Overview of the 12 Emergency Support Functions

ESF 1 *Transportation*: Provides for the coordination of federal transportation support to state and local governmental entities, voluntary organizations, and federal agencies requiring transportation capacity to perform disaster-assistance missions.

ESF 2 *Communications*: Provides federal telecommunications support to federal, state, and local response efforts following a disaster.

ESF 3 *Public Works and Engineering*: Provides public works and engineering support to assist the state(s) in meeting goals related to lifesaving, life protecting, and recovery efforts following a disaster.

ESF 4 *Fire Fighting*: Detects and suppresses wildland, rural, and urban fires resulting from, or occurring coincidentally with, a disaster.

ESF 5 *Information and Planning*: Collects, processes, and disseminates information about a potential or actual disaster or emergency to facilitate the overall activities of the federal government in providing response assistance. This ESF always deploys.

ESF 6 *Mass Care*: Coordinates efforts to provide sheltering, feeding, and emergency first aid following a disaster. Additional purpose is to operate a disaster welfare information system to collect, receive, and report information about the status of victims and assist family reunification; and to coordinate bulk distribution of emergency-relief supplies.

ESF 7 *Resource Support*: Provides logistical and resource support following a disaster.

ESF 8 *Health and Medical Services*: Provides coordinated assistance to supplement state and local resources in response to public health and medical needs following a significant disaster.

ESF 9 *Urban Search and Rescue*: Provides federal urban search and rescue teams capable of locating, extricating and providing for the immediate medical treatment of victims trapped in collapsed structures.

ESF 10 *Hazardous Materials*: Provides support to state and local governments in response to an actual or potential discharge and or release of hazardous materials.

ESF 11 *Food*: Identifies, secures, and arranges for the transportation of food assistance to affected areas following a disaster.

ESF 12 *Energy*: Helps restore the nation's energy systems following a disaster.

If desired, more information about each ESF can be found in detail in the Federal Response Plan.

ESF #8: Health and Medical Services

Although it is good to be aware of the entire federal response capability, we are primarily concerned here with ESF 8: Health and Medical Services. It is in this ESF that provision for the care of the deceased is discussed.

The primary agency for this ESF is the Department of Health and Human Services – United State Public Health Service.

Supporting agencies include:

- Department of Agriculture
- Department of Defense
- Department of Justice
- Department of Transportation
- Department of Veterans Affairs
- Agency for International Development
- American Red Cross
- Environmental Protection Agency
- Federal Emergency Management Agency
- General Services Administration
- National Communications System
- United States Postal Service

Support for ESF is categorized into the following functional areas:

a. Assessment of health and medical needs
b. Health surveillance
c. Medical care personnel
d. Health and medical equipment and supplies
e. Patient evacuations
f. In-hospital care
g. Food, drug, and medical safety devices
h. Worker health and safety
i. Radiological hazards
j. Chemical hazards
k. Biological hazards
l. Mental health
m. Public health information
n. Vector control
o. Potable water, wastewater, and solid waste disposal
p. Victim identification and mortuary services

Functional Area 16: Victim Identification and Mortuary Services

While it is good to be aware of all functional areas relating to ESF 8, the one with which we are primarily concerned here is Victim Identification and Mortuary Services. It is in this functional area that provisions for the care of the deceased are discussed.

The primary agency within the U.S. Public Health Service is the Office of Assistant Secretary of Health, Office of Emergency Preparedness – National Disaster Medical System.

The National Disaster Medical System provides victim identification and mortuary support through Disaster Mortuary Teams (DMORT.) There are 10 DMORTs that are aligned along the 10 FEMA regions. Each DMORT has a commander and assistant commander and comprises a variety of specialists, usually including:

- Forensic pathologists
- Medical examiners
- Coroners
- Forensic odontologists
- Forensic anthropologists
- Funeral directors
- Medical records technicians and transcribers
- Dental assistants
- X-ray technicians
- Mental health specialists
- Computer specialists
- Administrative support staff
- Security and investigative personnel

Members of the DMORT are all volunteers; when the Federal Response Plan or other mechanism to activate the DMORTs is initiated, the members become temporary federal government employees.

A fully equipped mobile mortuary is maintained by the DMORT. It is stored in Rockville, MD. It is transportable by air, sea, or land. It has been successfully deployed in support of mass fatality incidents.

DMORT have been active in many aviation incidents, natural disasters, and the Oklahoma City bombing. Many of the DMORT leaders have been instrumental and active in improving and shaping the mass fatality incident response in the U.S.

Summary

The U.S. has a highly developed disaster system that employs mass fatality incident specialists. Any state, commonwealth, or territory has the right to request and access the federal government's resources.

The federal government's mass fatality incident resources have evolved into a formal response structure capable of arriving and establishing complete mass fatality incident response. However, because the response structure was designed for major incidents, it is resource intensive with a large number of support personnel.

Over the past several years the federal government has successfully responded to numerous mass fatality incidents, including transportation accidents, natural disasters, and terrorist attacks.

He will wipe away all tears from their eyes. There will be no more death, no more grief or crying or pain. The old things have disappeared.

—*The Bible*, Book of Revelations, Chapter 21, Verse 4.

Appendix A:
Incident Response
Equipment

Supplies and equipment are listed by operational area, and certain items are listed in different areas, because they may be required simultaneously at different locations. Although I have specified computers in each case, consideration should be given to having an information technology specialist establish a complete Local Area Network, as well as e-mail capability.

Categories are:

- Search and Recovery
- Mass Fatality Incident Morgue
- Incident Management Operations Center
- Joint Family Assistance Center
- Joint Information Center

Equipment is listed by the common name of the item, or in rare cases, brand-name items that (in the author's opinion) are far superior.

The location column has been left blank for you to enter the item storage location, acquisition source, or other notes.

With limited budgets, I do not recommend that all jurisdictions maintain a mass fatality incident morgue. Instead, I suggest that neighboring jurisdictions work together to identify what resources they have on hand, what resources the next level of government has to support them, and likely sources to purchase or rent those needed items that are otherwise unavailable.

In the following checklists, you will find suggested items of equipment that you may want to consider for mass fatality incident response. Specialized equipment normally found with highly trained teams such as crash rescue, and heavy extraction teams is not listed as those teams usually come self equipped.

The quantity column is blank, that number is dependent upon the size and scope of the incident. I have also left the "Storage Location" blank so that you may write in the storage or acquisition location. I strongly encourage you as part of your pre-planning to identify the location of these items. I have also some blank lines for you to additional items as needed.

I have not included aftercare equipment such as would be used by licensed funeral directors. If a mass fatality incident morgue is configured to provide aftercare, local funeral directors or organizations such as the National Foundation for Mortuary Care should be contacted for equipment.

Search and Recovery Equipment List

Item	Individual Quantity	Storage Location
Bag, bio waste		
Bag, paper (various sizes)		
Bag, plastic (various sizes)		
Camera , set, 35mm		
Camera, digital, high resolution		
Camera, set, video		
Clipboard, aluminum, with 1" deep pocket		
Compass, lensatic		
Coveralls, extra large		
Coveralls, large		
Coveralls, medium		
Coveralls, small		
Cutters, bolt large		
Flags, pin yellow		
Flags, pin-blue		
Flags, pin-orange		
Flags, pin-red		
Global position system. handheld		
Gloves, leather men's work, large		
Gloves, leather men's work, medium		
Gloves, leather men's work, small		
Gloves, MAXXUS,® orthopedic, Size 8		
Gloves, MAXXUS,® orthopedic, Size 9		
Light, flashlight, non-spark, 3 "C" cell		
Link, snap connector, D-ring		
Litter, aluminum pole folding		
Litter, stokes		
Mask, anti-putrefaction		
Nails, 10-penny		
Notepad, graph		
Notepad, standard		
Paint, spray, blue		
Paint, spray, orange		
Paint, spray, red		
Paint, spray, yellow		
Pen, Uni-Ball, black		
Pen, Uni-Ball, red		
Pen, waterproof, black		
Pen, waterproof, red		
Pouch, human-remains, adult		
Pouch, human-remains, child		
Pouch, human-remains, water recovery		
Radio, hand held		
Range finder, electronic >50		
Range finder, electronic, <50		

Search and Recovery List cont'd. Item	Individual Quantity	Storage Location
Rope, nylon, 120' coil		
Sifters, w/ stands		
Stakes, metal engineering, 2'		
Stakes, metal engineering, 3'		
Stakes, metal engineering, 4'		
Stakes, wood, 3'		
Survey instrument, total station, complete		
Tag, toe, Tyvek®		
Tape measure, 100'		
Tape measure, 50'		
Tape, roll, barrier, biohazard		
Tape, roll, barrier, caution		
Tape, roll, masking		
Tool, ax		
Tool, hammer, hand		
Tool, hammer, sledge, 8-lb		
Tool, machete		
Tool, pickax		
Tool, pick handle		
Tool, rake, garden		
Tool, shovel, flat blade		
Tool, shovel, round blade		
Tool, trowel, small		
Twine, roll, cotton, 20 ply, (extra heavy duty), 300-yard		

Mass Fatality Incident Morgue Equipment

Item	Individual Quantity	Storage Location	Use
Bag, waste			Admin
Binder, 2"			Admin
Binder, 3"			Admin
Box, banker			Admin
Calendar			Admin
Card, identification blank			Admin
Cards, 3 x 5			Admin
Chair, folding			Admin
Clip, binder-medium			Admin
Clipboard			Admin
Computer, desktop			Admin
Copier, commercial			Admin
Cord, extension			Admin
Cutters, bolt small			Admin
Easel, stand			Admin
Folder, file			Admin
Label, dot-black			Admin
Label, dot-blue			Admin
Label, dot-green			Admin
Label, dot-red			Admin
Label, dot-white			Admin
Lamination pouches, card			Admin
Laminator, card			Admin
Light, flashlight, non-spark, 3 "c" cell			Admin
Map, (of incident area)			Admin
Marker, dry erase			Admin
Marker, highlighter			Admin
Monitor, computer			Admin
Pad, "post it"			Admin
Pad, legal			Admin
Pad, standard			Admin
Padlock, combination			Admin
Paper, 8-1/2" x 11"			Admin
Paper, pad easel			Admin
Paperclips			Admin
Pencil, sharpener			Admin
Pencils			Admin
Pens			Admin
Power supply, (ups)			Admin
Printer, laser			Admin
Protector, document			Admin
Punch, hole			Admin
Radios, hand held, 2-way			Admin
Rubber band			Admin
Ruler, 14"			Admin

Item	Individual Quantity	Storage Location	Use
Scissors			Admin
Shredder, paper			Admin
Staple, remover			Admin
Stapler			Admin
Staples			Admin
Table, folding			Admin
Tape, "scotch"			Admin
Tape, barrier			Admin
Thumbtacks			Admin
Anvil pruner			Anthro
Brush, stiff			Anthro
Flashlight, pen			Anthro
Forcep, fixation			Anthro
Forcep, gathering			Anthro
Forcep, straight			Anthro
Hemostat, jaw			Anthro
Hook, aneurysm			Anthro
Knife, butcher			Anthro
Magnifier, glasses			Anthro
Magnifier, glasses, headband			Anthro
Magnifier, hand 5"			Anthro
Magnifier, table mounted, lighted			Anthro
Ostrometric board			Anthro
Ring, donut			Anthro
Scalpel, blade (various sizes)			Anthro
Scalpel, handle (various sizes)Anthro			Anthro
Scissors, angular, tissue cutting			Anthro
Scissors, utility			Anthro
Tape. steel measuring 25'			Anthro
Autopsy diagrams (various)			Autopsy
Bag, visera			Autopsy
Blood tube, grey cap			Autopsy
Blood tube, purple cap			Autopsy
Blood tube, red cap			Autopsy
Bone cutter			Autopsy
Camera, lense 28 mm			Autopsy
Camera, 35 mm			Autopsy
Camera, battery			Autopsy
Camera, film 35 mm, asa 100			Autopsy
Camera, flash			Autopsy
Camera, flash, battery			Autopsy
Container, sealable glass			Autopsy
Cutter, ring			Autopsy
Forceps (various sizes)			Autopsy
Forceps, fixation			Autopsy
Hemostat			Autopsy
Hook, aneurysm			Autopsy

Item	Individual Quantity	Storage Location	Use
Knife, butcher			Autopsy
Magnifiers (various)			Autopsy
Mounting squares			Autopsy
Saw, arbor			Autopsy
Saw, arbor wrench			Autopsy
Saw, autopsy (stryker)			Autopsy
Saw, autopsy (stryker)			Autopsy
Scale, autopsy			Autopsy
Scalpel, blade (various)			Autopsy
Scalpel, handle (various)			Autopsy
Scissors, angler			Autopsy
Scissors, utility			Autopsy
Table, autopsy			Autopsy
Tape, steel measuring 25'			Autopsy
"Q-tip"			Dental
Brush, denture			Dental
Brush, toothbrush			Dental
Chart, dental			Dental
Flashlight, pen			Dental
Magnifier, glasses (loupe)			Dental
Magnifier, glasses, headband			Dental
Magnifier, hand 5"			Dental
Magnifier, table mounted, lighted			Dental
Mirror, cone socket			Dental
Mirror, cone socket, handle			Dental
Mouth prop			Dental
Scalpel, blade (various sizes)			Dental
Scalpel, handle (various sizes)			Dental
Scissors, angular, tissue cutting			Dental
Scissors, utility			Dental
Cleaning, supplies, various			General
Hose, water			General
Nozzle, water hose			General
Poles, support (for sheet)			General
Sheet, plastic (various sizes)			General
Bag, plastic (various sizes)			PE
Camera, lens 28 mm			PE
Camera, 35 mm			PE
Camera, battery			PE
Camera, film 35 mm, asa 100			PE
Camera, flash			PE
Camera, flash, battery			PE
Chain of custody forms			PE
Inventory forms			PE
Magnifier, hand 5"			PE
Magnifier, table mounted, lighted			PE
Scissors, utility			PE

Item	Individual Quantity	Storage Location	Use
Apron, neoprene			PPE
Bag, waste, biohazard			PPE
Containers, sharps			PPE
Cover, shoe			PPE
Covering, hair			PPE
Glasses, safety			PPE
Gloves, autopsy (various sizes)			PPE
Gloves, latex (various sizes)			PPE
Gloves, neoprene			PPE
Goggles			PPE
Label, biohazard			PPE
Mask, face			PPE
Respirator, filter (organic & formaldehyde)			PPE
Respirator, full face			PPE
Shield, face			PPE
Suit, coveralls, Tyvek® (various sizes)			PPE
Camera, polaroid (spectra)			Printing
Camera, polaroid lens, Close-up (spectra)			Printing
Camera, polaroid, film			Printing
Cutter, ring			Printing
Fingerprint cards			Printing
Magnifier, 3-1/2-x hand			Printing
Magnifier, glasses (loupe)			Printing
Magnifier, headband (loupe)			Printing
Nin powder, blue			Printing
Pads, portion (large & small)			Printing
Printing glass			Printing
Printing roller (finger & palm)			Printing
Printing spoon			Printing
Scalpel, blade (various)			Printing
Scalpel, handle (various)			Printing
Scissors, angular			Printing
Scissors, utility			Printing
Tubes, printing ink			Printing
X-ray imager, dental			X-ray
X-ray machine full body			X-ray
X-ray machine, dental			X-ray
X-ray, film dental			X-ray
X-ray, film developer			X-ray
X-ray, film full body			X-ray
X-ray, imager, full body			X-ray

Incident Management Operations Center Equipment

Item	Individual Quantity	Storage Location
Bag, waste		
Binder, 2"		
Binder, 3"		
Box, banker		
Calendar		
Card, identification blank		
Cards, 3 x 5		
Chair, folding		
Clip, binder-medium		
Clipboard		
Computer, desktop		
Copier, commercial		
Cord, extension		
Cutters, bolt, small		
Easel, stand		
Folder, file		
Label, dot-black		
Label, dot-blue		
Label, dot-green		
Label, dot-red		
Label, dot-white		
Laminator, card		
Lamination pouches, card		
Light, flashlight, non-spark, 3 "C" Cell		
Marker, dry erase		
Marker, highlighter		
Map, (of incident area)		
Monitor, computer		
Pad, "Post It"		
Pad, legal		
Pad, standard		
Padlock, combination		
Paper, 8-1/2" x 11"		
Paper, pad easel		
Paperclips		
Pens		
Pencils		
Pencil, sharpener		
Podium, briefing		
Pointer, briefing		
Power supply, (UPS)		
Printer, laser		
Protector, document		
Punch, hole		
Radios, hand held, 2-way		
Rubber bands		

Item	Individual Quantity	Storage Location
Ruler, 14"		
Scissors		
Shredder, paper		
Staple remover		
Stapler		
Staples		
Table, folding		
Tape, "Scotch"		
Tape, barrier		
Thumbtacks		

Joint Family Assistance Center Equipment List

Item	Individual Quantity	Storage Location
Bag, waste		
Binder, 2"		
Binder, 3"		
Box, banker		
Calendar		
Card, identification blank		
Cards, 3 x 5		
Chair, folding		
Clip, binder-medium		
Clipboard		
Computer, desktop		
Copier, commercial		
Cord, extension		
Cutters, bolt, small		
Easel, stand		
Folder, file		
Label, dot-black		
Label, dot-blue		
Label, dot-green		
Label, dot-red		
Label, dot-white		
Laminator, card		
Lamination pouches, card		
Light, flashlight, non-spark, 3 "C" Cell		
Marker, dry erase		
Marker, highlighter		
Map, (of incident area)		
Monitor, computer		
Pad, "Post It"		
Pad, legal		
Pad, standard		
Padlock, combination		
Paper, 8-1/2" x 11"		
Paper, pad easel		
Paperclips		
Pens		
Pencils		
Pencil, sharpener		
Podium, briefing		
Pointer, briefing		
Power supply, (UPS)		
Printer, laser		
Protector, document		
Punch, hole		
Radios, hand held, 2-way		

Item	Individual Quantity	Storage Location
Rubber bands		
Ruler, 14"		
Scissors		
Shredder, paper		
Staple remover		
Stapler		
Staples		
Table, folding		
Tape, "Scotch"		
Tape, barrier		
Thumbtacks		

Joint Information Center Equipment List

Item	Individual Quantity	Storage Location
Bag, waste		
Binder, 2"		
Binder, 3"		
Box, banker		
Calendar		
Card, identification blank		
Cards, 3 x 5		
Chair, folding		
Clip, binder-medium		
Clipboard		
Computer, desktop		
Copier, commercial		
Cord, extension		
Cutters, bolt, small		
Easel, stand		
Folder, file		
Label, dot-black		
Label, dot-blue		
Label, dot-green		
Label, dot-red		
Label, dot-white		
Laminator, card		
Lamination pouches, card		
Light, flashlight, non-spark, 3 "C" Cell		
Marker, dry erase		
Marker, highlighter		
Map, (of incident area)		
Monitor, computer		
Pad, "Post It"		
Pad, legal		
Pad, standard		
Padlock, combination		
Paper, 8-1/2" x 11"		
Paper, pad easel		
Paperclips		
Pens		
Pencils		
Pencil, sharpener		
Podium, briefing		
Pointer, briefing		
Power supply, (UPS)		
Printer, laser		
Protector, document		
Punch, hole		
Radios, hand held, 2-way		

Item	Individual Quantity	Storage Location
Rubber bands		
Ruler, 14"		
Scissors		
Shredder, paper		
Staple remover		
Stapler		
Staples		
Table, folding		
Tape, "Scotch"		
Tape, barrier		
Thumbtacks		

Appendix B:
Suggested Resources

When training for and establishing a mass fatality incident response plan, I recommend that you consider contacting the local representatives of the groups listed below. Enter their contact information below, and keep it for a ready reference. You may find that many of their members will have had experience in some or all areas of a mass fatality incident response.

Local Organizations

State Funeral Directors Association

Contact Name:

_____

Contact Telephone Number:

_____

24 Hour Contact Telephone Number:

_____

Type of assistance organization is willing to provide:

_____
_____
_____

State Emergency Manager's Office
Contact Name:

Contact Telephone Number:

24-Hour Contact Telephone Number:

Type of assistance organization is willing to provide:

Local Search and Rescue Group
Contact Name:

Contact Telephone Number:

24-Hour Contact Telephone Number:

Type of assistance organization is willing to provide:

Local Medical Examiner or Coroners Association
Contact Name:

Contact Telephone Number:

24-Hour Contact Telephone Number:

Type of assistance organization is willing to provide:

_____

_____

_____

Nearest National Guard or Army Reserve Unit

Contact Name:

_____

Contact Telephone Number:

_____

24-Hour Contact Telephone Number:

_____

Type of assistance organization is willing to provide:

_____

_____

_____

Local Red Cross/Red Crescent

Contact Name:

_____

Contact Telephone Number:

_____

24-Hour Contact Telephone Number:

_____

Type of assistance organization is willing to provide:

_____

_____

_____

Local Dental Association
Contact Name:

_____

Contact Telephone Number:

_____

24-Hour Contact Telephone Number:

_____

Type of assistance organization is willing to provide:

_____
_____
_____

Nearest University With Forensic Anthropologist
Contact Name:

_____

Contact Telephone Number:

_____

24-Hour Contact Telephone Number:

_____

Type of assistance organization is willing to provide:

_____
_____
_____

National Organizations

FEMA Director
Contact Name:

Contact Telephone Number:

24-Hour Contact Telephone Number:

DMORT Region Commander
Contact Name:

Contact Telephone Number:

24-Hour Contact Telephone Number:

NFMC Trustee
Contact Name:

Contact Telephone Number:

24-Hour Contact Telephone Number:

Suggested Readings

In addition to establishing a relationship with the contacts listed above, I recommend that you consider adding the following books to your professional library. None of the books focus strictly on mass fatality incidents, they do, however, provide useful information that is helpful in responding to one.

FEMA Catalogue, which lists numerous books available at no charge:

FEMA Publications
P.O. Box 2012
Jessup, Maryland 20794-2012

Suggested publications:
    Federal Response Plan: Executive Overview, FEMA 229(1)
    The Federal Response Plan Including Changes, FEMA 229

OSHA Publications
US Department of Labor OSHA Publications
P.O. Box 37535
Washington, Dc, 20013-7535

Suggested publications:
    Bloodborne Pathogens and Dental Workers – OSHA 3129
    Bloodborne Pathogens and Emergency Responders – OSHA 3130
    Chemical Hazard Communication – OSHA 3084
    Occupational Exposure to Bloodborne Pathogens – OSHA 3127
    Personal Protective Equipment – OSHA 3077

Further Reading:

Caplan, Yale H., Ed., *Medicolegal Death Investigations, Treatises in the Forensic Sciences*, The Forensic Sciences Foundation Press, 1997.

Geberth, Vernon J., *Practical Homicide Investigation, Tactics, Procedures, and Forensic Techniques*, 3rd ed., CRC, Boca Raton FL, 1996.

Ursano, Robert J., Brian G. McCaughey, and Carol S. Fullerton, Eds., *Individual and Community Responses to Trauma and Disaster: The Structure of Human Chaos*, Cambridge University Press, New York, 1994.

Haglund, William D. and Marcella H. Sorg, Eds., *Forensic Taphonomy: The Postmortem Fate of Human Remains*, CRC, Boca Raton, FL, 1997.

Suggested Training Programs

Medicolegal Death Investigator, A Systematic Training Program for the Professional Death Investigator, Steven C. Clark, Mary Fran Ernst, William D. Haglund, and Jeffrey M. Jentzen, Occupational Research and Assessment, Inc., 124 Elm Street, Big Rapids, Michigan 49307, 1996.

Medicolegal Death Investigators Course (Basic and Master's), St. Louis University School of Medicine, St. Louis, MO, 63104, Contact Mary Fran Ernst.

National Association POLs

Critical Incident Stress Debriefing Team

American Critical Incident Stress Foundation (410) 313-2473

FBI Disaster Team

(Contact local FBI office to request the team)

National Association of Medical Examiners (314) 577-8298

(Can provide contacts and some planning material)

Index

R

Radios, 78
Raw data, 83
Receiving operations, initial, 141
Receiving station, 97, 193
Reception station, 165, 182
Recognition and awards, 43
Recovery
    operations, 203
    overview, 69
    personnel, 76
    staging area, 82
Reentry, 45
Regional Operations Center (ROC), 203
Release area, 124
Remains, xiii
    comingled, 79, 80
    disposition of unidentified, 171
    intact, 83, 85
    photographing of, 105
    placement of into temporary refriger-
        ated holding, 99
    receiving of, 98
Resources, suggested, 227–233
    local organizations, 227–230
    local dental association, 230
    local medical examiner or coroners
        association, 228–229
    local Red Cross/Red Crescent, 229
    local search and rescue group, 228
    nearest National Guard or Army
        Reserve unit, 229
    nearest university with forensic
        anthropologist, 230
    state funeral directors association,
        227–228
    national organizations, 231
    DMORT region commander, 231
    FEMA director, 231
    NFMC trustee, 231
Responder protection, 47–66
    biological hazards, 47–48
    communicating hazards to
        employees, 50
    engineering controls, 51
    exposure incident, 55–57
    hazardous materials, 58
    housekeeping, 54–55
    labeling, 55

mass fatality responder liability, 65–66
methods of control, 51
personal protective equipment, 53
preventive measures, 51
recommended compliance strategies,
    60–65
mass fatality incident exposure control,
    61–65
mass fatality incident morgue, 60
mass fatality incident site, 60
training requirements, 60–61
recordkeeping, 57–58
threat, 49
who is covered, 49
work practice controls, 52
written exposure-control plan, 49–50
written hazardous communication
    plan, 59
Response actions, questioning, 177
Response Operations, 203
Right to know, 59
Robert T. Stafford Disaster Relief and
    Emergency Act, 199
ROC, see Regional Operations Center

S

Sanitary services, 196
SCO, see State Coordinating Officer
Search
    basics, 70
    overview, 67
    patterns, 73
    resources, 90
    sequence, 75, 135
    team
    assembling and briefing of, 76
    photographers, 76
Search and recovery operations, 67–91
    gridding, 82–91
    buildings/ships, 85–86
    establishing additional grid squares, 89
    establishing grid square markers, 88–89
    limited-line-of-site incidents, 85
    open terrain incidents, 83–95
    recovery overview, 69
    search basics, 69–75
        aircraft accident, ground recovery, 70

V

Vaccinations, 62
Victim identification, 209
Video viewing center, 170
Viewable remains, xiii
Volunteer SAR teams, 91

W

Warehouse considerations, 139
Water recovery, aircraft accident, 70
Westing, 83
Windows Identification (WinID), 118
WinID, see Windows Identification

Work
    areas, defined, 63
    practice controls, 52
Writing supplies, 78
Written exposure control plan, 49, 55,
    61, 62, 64
Written hazardous communication plan, 59

X

X-ray
    of large tissue mass, 111, 112
    station, 110